A Masterclass in Antique Furniture

An illustrated guide to identifying American, English, Dutch and French antique furniture, clocks and musical instruments

Published by Triangle Circle Square press

ISBN-13: 978-1-387-76430-3

© Thomas M. Clark 2016

Contents

Introduction

This guidebook to antique furnishings aspires to showcase the typical qualities of period furniture distinguished by three key aspects:

Firstly we have the country of manufacture; the geographical distance between France, the Netherlands, England and the United States meant individual talents and manufacturers were each placed in environments allowing the creation of very varied items. At the time they made such designs, there were few illustrations to sway their able hands. There were certainly no Internet to provide ready access and inspiration with a few clicks of a computer mouse, and long distance travel to other showrooms was difficult in a time predating cheap mass travel. The manufacturer did not work in a vacuum, but nor was he able to collate designs as one might peruse a supermarket for groceries, or browse holidays in a travel brochure, or 'network' vociferously.

**Empire style meets neoclassicism in the Empress Josephine's apartment -
Image: Moonik**

Secondly, we have the chronology – the period from the 17th to the 19th century was, for many a connoisseur of decorative furniture, the very zenith of all fine craftsmanship. In an era where even the term 'artisanal' is applied with reckless abandon to everything, it is easy to overlook the achievements of the individual makers and designers whom elevated that term to a true, sublime meaning. The common circumstance of individual pieces creation was a shared education – differences were built by the wit and inventions of each maker, with sometimes blissful results stunning the monarchs, rulers and commercial grandees of these eras, who became patrons, gracefully showering wealth upon the talent that so impressed them.

Lastly, we've the individual circumstances and facts of each era. A French maker aspiring to decorate the court of the monarch of the time would make a vastly different chair, cabinet or bed than a Dutch or English furniture maker immersed in the exotic, faraway locales which all Europe became immersed in during the colonial era. No matter how resolute, no furniture maker's spirit could ward off the pressures and circumstances of his life – whether a lot or a little, his locality and the fancies of his peers would creep into his design. Influences of the distant past, as in neoclassical design, would further find their voice and place in the furnishings.

Figure French harpsichord by Pleyel, Wolff, Lyon & Cie - Image: Morn the Gorn

This book superficially resembles the annotated catalogue: large, pictorial representations find significant descriptions alongside them. Where the auction house theme departs however is where I have been sure to include individual anecdotes surrounding an item's creation, be it significant letters of the time or a narrative of the poignant historical events. The major furniture makers all receive due mention, for it is knowledge of these that every antique enthusiast or professional has as bedrock to his authority. Unlike a catalogue, I omit all valuations save for a few dating to the eras concerned.

The John Whipple House contains many superb examples of colonial furniture - Image: John Phelan

The concluding parts focus upon clocks and musical instruments. These two areas are something of a curiosity for the niche collector, to be viewed in complement to our overall focus upon furniture: a good timepiece and music would very commonly sit with furnishings. A fourth element – one of technological progress – is in full evidence here; the advances and increases in intricacy both of the mechanical clock and of the families of musical instruments would manifest in their designs.

I confess to understatement on the final pages: the handles, feet and other extremities of furniture are often the most pivotally differentiated parts. A keen collector and seller of antique furnishings must develop an obsessive scrutiny of these: they represent the portions most vulnerable to damage, to overzealous polishing, or forgery by the unscrupulous. If you aspire to purchase or trade in items, do not forget the details in this finale.

At the conclusion of this book, you can creditably call yourself informed – nothing, however, replaces the actual examination of these objects in person. While I dislike the term 'primer', that is what this guidebook does – readies you for the storied past, the history, the subtleties of design, and the attention to detail which underpins the antiques market. It makes pains to immerse you in the past which birthed these furnishings, while never losing the sight of each piece's defining characteristics.

Let us begin our examination now with an overview of old oak and leather furnishings, with a miniature glossary of sorts to clarify the terms and jargon we antique dealers use so extensively.

Thomas M. Clark, Spring 2016

Antique Oak and Leather Furnishings

WITH THE revival of interest in all "antiques," which is so widely spread at this time, any of us who chance to own an old piece of furniture feel an added degree of affection for it if we can give it an approximate date and assign it to a maker or a country. There is much good old furniture in the United States, chiefly of Spanish, Dutch and English make, though there are constant importations of other makes, notably French, since it is recognized on all sides that Americans are becoming the collectors of the world. Our public museums are gradually filling with works of art presented by broad-minded citizens, while the private galleries are rich and increasing every day.

To keep pace with these possessions, furniture from old palaces and manor-houses is being hauled forth and set up again in our New World homes. Indeed, whole interiors have been removed from ancient dwellings, and the superb carvings of other days become the ornaments of modern

This particular Venetian example, dating to the 18th century, escaped exportation and today rests in the Museum of Naples, Italy - Image: Karl

houses, like the gilded oak panels from the Hotel Montmorency which were built into the Deacon House in Boston, or like Mrs. Gardiner's Venetian carved wood which decorates the Boston Fens.

Oak panelling, like everything else, passed through various periods and styles. In Queen Elizabeth's time the panels were carried to within about two feet of the cornice; then, after some years, there came a division into lower and upper panelling, the upper beginning at about the height of the back of a chair from the floor. Pictures became more common, and they were frequently let into the upper panelling, and then it was discarded altogether, only the lower half or dado being retained. This, too, after some years, became old-fashioned, and the board known as skirting, or base-board, was all that was left of the handsome sheathing which extended from the floor almost to the ceiling. This old oak panelling was entirely without polish or varnish of any kind, and grew with years and dust almost black in colour. Sometimes it was inlaid with other woods, and often it was made for the rooms where it was placed. Where the panels are carved, they are generally bought in that state and set in plain framework by the household joiner. If, however, the frame is carved and the panels plain, they were made to suit the taste and purse of the owner of the mansion. Oak panelling took the place of the arras, tapestry hangings, and crude woodwork of earlier times. Of course it was adopted by the rich and luxurious, for it rendered more air-tight the draughty buildings.

Old Oak Bedstead

The oldest furniture was made of oak, more or less carved, whether of Spanish, Italian, Dutch, or English make. The multiplication of objects which we consider necessary as "furnishings" were pleasingly absent, and chests used as receptacles for clothes or linens, for seats by day and beds by night, with a few beds also of carved oak, and tables, made up the chief articles of domestic use.

Even the very word "furniture" itself is of obscure origin and was used formerly, as now, to describe the fittings of houses, churches, and other buildings.

There are a few terms applied to furniture referring either to its decoration or process of manufacture with which it is well to become acquainted. They are given here in the order of their importance.

Veneering is the process of coating common wood with slices of rare and costly woods fastened down with glue by screw presses made to fit the surface to be covered. It was first used in the reign of William and Mary, in the last decade of the seventeenth century. Until that time furniture had been made of solid wood. Veneer of this early period, particularly burr-walnut veneer, was about one sixteenth of an inch thick, and was sometimes applied to oak. Chippendale, Hepplewhite, and Sheraton used mahogany and satin-wood both solid and for veneers. When used as veneers they were all hand-cut, as they are in all high-class furniture to-day. It was not till the late Georgian period that machinery for cutting veneer was first used, and slices were produced one thirty-second of an inch in thickness. Most of the cheaper kinds of modern furniture are veneered.

Marquetry is veneer of different woods, forming a mosaic of ornamental designs. In the early days of the art, figure subjects, architectural designs, and interiors were often represented in this manner.

Rococo, made up from two French words meaning rock and shells, *roequaille et coquaille*, is a florid style of ornamentation which was in vogue in the latter part of the eighteenth century.

Buhl, or *Boulle*, is inlaid work with tortoise-shell or metals in arabesques or cartouches. It derived its name from Boule, a French wood-carver who brought it to its highest perfection.

Ormolu refers to designs in brass mounted upon the surface of the wood. This metal was given an exceedingly brilliant colour by the use of less zinc and more copper than is commonly used in the composition of brass, and was sometimes still further made bright by the use of varnish and lacquer.

Baroque. This word, which was derived from the Portuguese *baroco*, meant originally a large irregular pearl. At first the term was used only by jewellers, but it gradually became technically applied to describe a kind of ornament which became popular on furniture early in the nineteenth century, after the rage for the classic had passed. It consisted of a wealth of ornament lavished in an unmeaning manner merely for display; and scrolls, curves, and designs from leaves were used to cover pieces, making them lack beauty and that grace which comes from pure and simple lines.

Lacquer is coloured or opaque varnish applied to metallic objects as well as wood. The name is obtained from "resin lac," the material which is used as the base of all lacquers. In the East Indies the whole surface of wooden objects, large and small, is covered with bright-coloured lacquers. The Japanese lacquers are the finest that are made. They excel in the variety and exquisite perfection of this style of work, and under their skilful manipulation it becomes one of the choicest forms of decorative art. The most highly prized lacquer is on a gold ground, some specimens of which reached Europe in the time of Louis XV.

Japanning. This style of treating wood and metal derives its name from the fact of its being an imitation of the famous lacquering of Japan, although the latter is prepared with entirely different materials and processes, and is in every way much more durable, brilliant, and beautiful than any European "Japan work." This latter process is done in clear transparent varnishes, or in black or colours, but the black japan is the most common. By japanning a very brilliant polished surface may be secured, which is more durable than ordinary painted or varnished work. It is usually applied to small articles of wood, to clock-faces, papier-maché, etc.

Joined furniture. All the parts are joined by mortise and tenon, no nails or glue being used. This method prevents the parts from warping or springing, as so much of the modern machine-made furniture does.

The image shows an ancient carved-oak bed of the time of Queen Elizabeth, with grotesque carvings on the headboard in Renaissance style, which is said to have been introduced into England by Holbein. This bed has an interesting history. It belongs to the Herricks of Beaumanor Park, and came to them from Professor Babington, of St. John's College, Cambridge, England. He inherited it from his father, whose ancestors kept the "Blue Boar" inn at Leicester, where Richard III slept the night before the battle of Bosworth Field, in August, 1485. This has always been called "King Richard's Bed," and many learned antiquaries have waxed eloquent for and against this assumption. Mr. Henry Shaw, author of "Specimens of Early Furniture," published in 1836, says it is a good specimen of the modern four-poster of Elizabeth's time, the more ancient beds being without foot-posts. In fact the earlier beds were mere couches. As more luxury was demanded they grew larger, counterpanes were made of the richest materials, gorgeously embroidered with the arms and badges of their owners, and from their great cost and imperishable character descended from one generation to another. They provided employment, too, for the lady of the castle and her bower maidens, who had no end of leisure which had to be filled in some way, and which dragged along for many a long year, broken only by the chance visit of a wandering hawker or my lord's return from the wars.

Olive Wood Chest

Hollingbourne Manor, in Kent, is one of the old mansions still standing which was built in Queen Elizabeth's time. The manor was originally owned by Sir Thomas Culpeper, and his initials appear in many places about the house. In the great hall the fireplace has an iron back with the initials "T. C." and the date 1683 wrought in it. The present owner, Mr. Gerald Arbuthnot, has preserved the old-time atmosphere as much as possible, and in connection with home-made tapestry the "needle-room" is especially interesting. In that room the four Ladies Culpeper, daughters of that John, Lord Culpeper, who was exiled for his devotion to King Charles, spent so much of their time making tapestry that one of the sisters became blind from the effects of her close application. Among the pieces of the handiwork of the four sisters preserved is a magnificent altar-cloth which they presented to the parish church. For two centuries and a half a needle left by the fingers of the

10

worker remained sticking in the corner of the cloth, but it was stolen about two years ago by some one of a party of antiquarians visiting the Manor.

In Mr. Shaw's book already quoted are many items concerning these great and handsome beds, which were often the finest pieces of furniture in the castle or manor, and from the safe seclusion of which the king or great lord received the homage of his vassals.

The bed and bedstead were sometimes classed separately, but in many inventories the former word covers the bedstead and all its furnishings. The fittings of the bed were well in keeping with the fine carved woodwork, and were of softest feathers or down. Sheets of linen, and rugs or blankets of fine wool, were covered by a cloth woven of samite, damask, or heavy with gold threads.

Richard, Earl of Arundel, in 1392, left to Philippa, his second wife,—

—"a blue bed marked with my arms and the arms of my late wife, also the hangings of the hall, which were lately made in London, of blue tapestry with red roses, with the arms of my sons, the Earl Marshall, Lord Charlton, and Mons. Willm. Beauchamp; to my son Richard, a standing bed called "Clove"; also a bed of silk embroidered with the arms of Arundel and Warren quarterly; to my dear son Thomas, my blue bed of silk embroidered with greffins; to my daughter Margaret my blue bed."

Not many earls had so great a store of worldly goods.

In 1434 Joanne, Lady Bergavenny, devises—

—"a bed of gold swans, with tapettar of green tapestry, with bunches and flowers of diverse colours; and two pair of sheets of Raynes; a pair of fustian, six pairs of other sheets; six pairs of blankets; six mattrasses; six pillows; and with cushions and bancoves that longen with the bed aforesaid."

This was only one bed of six specified by this lady, several being of velvet, silk, and one of "bande kyn," a rich and splendid stuff of gold thread and silk, still farther enriched with embroidery. Before the cloth spread or counterpane the covering was of fur. It was also the fashion in these primitive times to name the beds, like that specified "Clove" in the Earl of Arundel's inventory, sometimes with the names of flowers, sometimes with those of the planets or of birds. The beds were surmounted with testers or canopies of rich silk edged with fringes, and suspended from the rafters of the room by silk cords. There were side-curtains also, and much carving on the headboard, while the foot-posts, as we have said, are wanting in the earliest beds, prior to the year 1500. Mr. Shaw goes on to say that there are very few beds still extant which date before Elizabethan times, and that the most ancient he met with was of the time of Henry VIII., and belonged to a clergyman of Blackheath who bought it out of an old manor-house. The posts and back are elaborately carved in Gothic style, but the cornice is missing.

Of Elizabethan times there are several noted beds extant, the finest of them being known as the "Great Bed of Ware" mentioned by Shakespeare in "Twelfth Night." It is seven feet high and ten feet square. There is one in the South

Kensington Museum, London, more richly carved than the one we show, and having in addition a carved foot-board. This bed is dated 1593.

The curtains and hangings which have in our day become mere ornaments were during the Elizabethan period most necessary. Windows unglazed, and rude walls unplastered, or at best hung with tapestry, permitted drafts to wander through the sleeping-rooms, so that the curtains were closely drawn at night for actual protection. At best in many a castle or dwelling of the wealthy but one bed would be found, and that belonged to the lord and lady, the rest of the family taking their rest on rugs or cushions bestowed on the floor, or on chests or settees, or even on tables.

Old Oak Chest

There are also found, though rarely, oak tables of this period, or perhaps a little later, heavily carved along the sides, and with ponderous turned legs and plain stout braces. These tables, perhaps the earliest approach to a sideboard, are so long that they have six legs, the top seldom being less than twelve feet in length. One we refer to was found recently in an old barn in England, where it had lain since the neighbouring manor-house had been pulled down in 1760. While its condition was good,—that is, needing no restoring,—it had become nearly black and almost fossilized from exposure. It is now used as a sideboard by the vicar of the parish who found it in its lowly estate, and on it stand pewter and plate, also antiques from the neighbourhood. Such treasures can seldom be found here, certainly not any that have lain concealed since 1760.

After the Elizabethan period the next one of importance may be called Jacobean. James I. encouraged his people to use chairs instead of stools. It was not long before settles, lounges, and "scrowled chairs," the latter inlaid with coloured woods, crowded out the stools of former days, and the idea of enriching the useful became the interest of the skilled workman, and utility was no longer the measure of value. Stools, to be sure, were still used, but they had heavy cushions of brocade, or worked stuff, or velvet, and were hung around with a rich fringe and with gimp, fastened with fancy nails. The arm-chairs of this period, a fashion introduced from Venice, had the legs in a curved X shape across the front, and chairs are still extant which were used by James I. himself. These chairs, which are all somewhat similar in design, were rendered still more comfortable by a loose cushion which could be adapted to the inclination of the sitter. The bedsteads of the period were also smothered in draperies, the tester trimmed with rows upon rows of fringe, the head-boards, carved and gilded, being about the only woodwork allowed to show.

As we have said, the earliest wood used, at least in northern England, seems to have been oak. At the close of the sixteenth century there was furniture decorated with inlays of different coloured woods, marbles, agate, or lapis lazuli. Ivory carved and inlaid, carved and gilded wood, metals and tortoise-shell, were used also in making the

Chest With One Drawer

sumptuous furniture of the Renaissance. The greatest elegance of form and detail was observed during this century, and it declined noticeably all over Europe, during the seventeenth century. The framework became heavy and bulky and the details coarse. Silver furniture made in Spain and Italy was used in the courts of the French and English kings. Then came the carved and gilded furniture which received its greatest perfection in Italy, though it was made throughout Europe till late in the eighteenth century.

Second only to the bed in importance as an item of household furnishing was the chest, a seat by day, a bed by night, and a storehouse of valuables always. It usually stood at the foot of the bed, possibly so that it could not be pilfered at night without the owner's knowledge. Some chests, heavily made, provided with locks and bound with iron, held all the worldly wealth of the owner, as well as his papers and deeds. Before the time of James I. bills of exchange were not used, and the actual coin passed in all transactions. Italy was the first country to establish banks, the money-dealers of Florence practising banking as early as the thirteenth century. Holland followed their example, and in 1609 the Bank of Amsterdam was founded, but kept in its coffers the actual coin paid in, being merely a repository for safe keeping.

England had no bank until the seventeenth century, when this business was undertaken by the goldsmiths of London. The Bank of England was not founded until 1694. It can be easily seen how necessary a part of the household goods a stout chest for valuables was, especially in remote parts of the country, where access to the cities was not easy. Not alone in houses was the chest a necessary article; one or more were a part of every church's furniture, and in them were kept the vestments, church linen, the plate, and other valuables.

There is a lawsuit mentioned in the Court Records of New Amsterdam, where one of two sisters living at Jericho, Long Island, about 1647, sues a neighbour for coming into their house and breaking into her chest, which was in her bedroom, and stealing from it several measures of wheat which were stored therein, as well as some coins which were in the till.

Oak Chest on Frame - English

The wearing-apparel of the family also was kept in these chests, and for years before her marriage the daughter of the house was employed in filling one up with linen spun and woven through all the different processes from the flax, the size and fullness of the chest often proving quite a factor in the marriage negotiations.

The chests of the Jacobean time, enriched with mouldings, panellings, and drop ornaments, are by no means unknown in America. They are furnished with drawers, cupboards, and then drawers above, making them massive and useful pieces of furniture. They stand upon large round legs, and the handles to drawers and cupboards are drops. In Italy marriage chests were beautifully painted, often by famous masters, and sometimes gilded as well. In Holland the chests were carved or inlaid; and many of these, owing to the commercial relations between England and Holland, found their way into the former country and thence to America, in addition to those brought directly from the Low Countries. Chests were used as trunks by travelers long before Shakespeare's time, and he makes a chest play an important part in "Cymbeline."

In the early days of the American colonies, when the settlers sent back to England for comforts not procurable in America, these were generally despatched in chests for safe keeping and to preserve their contents. The following letter shows a lady's desire to get hold of her property which had been unduly detained. Lady Moody was a member in 1643 of the Colony of Massachusetts, but, "being taken with the error of denying baptism to infants, was dealt with by many of the elders," As she persisted in her "error" she was persuaded by friends, in order to avoid further trouble, to move to the New Netherlands. This she did, and it is noted by the Rev. Thomas Cobbett, of Lynn, that "Lady Moody is to sitt down on Long Island, from under civil and church watch, among the Dutch."

Later she became a warm friend of the younger Winthrop, and many letters passed between them. The following was written in 1649:

"Wurthi Sur:

My respective love to you, remembering and acknowledging your many kindnesses and respect to me. I have written divers lines to you, but I doubt you have not received it. At present being in haste I can not unlay myselfe, but my request is y^t you will be pleased by this note, if in your wisdom you see not a convenienter opertunity to send me those things y^t Mr Throgmorton bought for me, and I understand are with you, for I am in great need of y^e, together with Mark Lucas's chest and other things.

"So, with my respective love to you and your wife and Mrs Locke remembered, hoping you and they with your children are in helth, I rest; committing you to ye protection of ye Almighty. Pray remember my necessity in this thing.

DEBORAH MOODY."

Chests are to be found in the well-settled as well as in out-of-the-way corners, and of Dutch, English, and American make. The Dutch, broadly speaking, are more common in the neighbourhood of New York, Albany, and other places settled by these pioneers from Holland, while the English-made ones, many of them, are to be found in New England, and scattered over the Eastern States as well, since in the past year I have seen two fine ones, both found in the western part of New York State. The very earliest chests which were among the effects of our first settlers are very plain affairs, hardly more than boxes mounted on simple sawed legs. They were all furnished with locks, and generally with rude handles, and we can well conceive the motley array of household and personal "stuff" which came over in them. Elder Brewster's chest is in the Memorial Hall at Plymouth, and is just such a plain box on legs as has been described.

Though there were many oak chests undoubtedly brought over during these early years, there were also many of pine, and, being plain and cheap receptacles, more easily damaged than if of harder wood, they gave way to better and more ornate pieces as soon as the family fortunes warranted it.

In Flanders were made many fronts of chests only, quite elaborately carved, and sent to England, there to be fitted with the other parts. Among the guilds the chest-makers bore an important part, as chests, particularly of churches, were sometimes fastened with two locks, and the lock plates were often very highly and handsomely wrought. Of later years chests of every degree of elegance and beauty have found their way to America; some covered with carving of the florid style of the Renaissance, some still showing traces of the fine gilding with which they were covered. Even some of historic interest are owned here, such as the carved chest of olive-wood said to have belonged to the Stuarts, and brought to this country by a member of the family who fled to Virginia after the beheading of Charles I. It remained in the possession of a family named Stuart till recently, and was bought by its present owner, Miss C. F. Marsh, of Clermont-on-the-James. This chest, though restored as to its feet, is remarkable on account of the decorations on the inside of its lid, which are unusual in that place, and from the fact that they are done in burnt work as well as carving. A portrait of James I. occupies the centre, and there are carved panels on either side depicting the "Judgment of Solomon." On the top of the lid the arms of the Stuarts are burnt in, while the front is decorated with panels of castles and warriors, and above the middle panel are the British lions supporting the royal arms. This chest is about six feet in length, twenty-four inches high, and

Spanish Leather Chair

twenty-two inches wide. The plantation on which it was found belonged to Captain John Smith in 1610. Its real value was quite unknown to those who possessed it. It was sold at auction, and was bought by a German farmer for a feed-box, on account of its strength. He carted it home, and was so satisfied with his bargain that he was quite unwilling to sell. It is made of eight-inch planks of olive-wood, cut several centuries ago in Palestine.

Nor is this the only chest of this description in the country. In Memorial Hall, Philadelphia, is one very similar to it but in a perfect state of preservation, with the original ball feet and more ornate twisted wrought-iron handles. The style of decoration on the two chests is quite similar, they are both made of olive-wood, but the wrought-iron handles are much handsomer on the Philadelphia chest than on the Stuart one. It has, however, no carving on the inside of the lid; the four panels of carving are enclosed with a moulding; but the lions rampant are very well done, and there are figures in cavalier costume on the panels. While, of course, elegant chests like these are most uncommon, it is the less ornate specimens which prove the most interesting, because there is more likelihood of our becoming possessed of them.

Our image of the chest of one drawer represents a good specimen of one of these early chests. It is of English make, entirely of oak, the boards of the bottom being as heavy and solid as lead. The top is a heavy plank of oak with a fine grain. The chest is panelled within and has one till. The lock is modern, and some nails have been driven to hold the chest together, for the back legs as well as the sides are worm-eaten. This chest is three feet nine inches long, twenty-eight inches high, and twenty inches wide, and is in good condition save for the nails. Its date is about the last quarter of the seventeenth century. It was found in New York State and belongs to Mr. W. M. Hoyt of Rochester. While oak and pine were the most common materials for these chests, olive-wood was sometimes used, as we have seen, and sometimes the panels were of cedar, and the ornaments of some of the softer woods, like pine or maple, coloured and stained to imitate ebony. American walnut came into use late in the seventeenth century, but, although used in furniture and popular as a veneer, it was not used for chests. Cypress wood was also in demand as a material for chests, the aromatic smell keeping off the pest of housekeepers, the moth. In summer time the heavy woollen tapestries and woollen clothes of the family were stowed away, and the former, at least, from their cost and the labour expended upon them, had to be carefully protected.

The roughest sort of a chest was called a "standard," and in it were packed the more perishable movables and furniture; and in moving from one residence to another these standards were carried by pack-horses or on rude carts. Chinese chests of teak-wood, lacquer, or cedar are very rarely met with, though you will sometimes see them in old homes in England, where some ancestor of the family followed the sea.

The inventory of the estate of Colonel Francis Epes, of Henrico County, Virginia, dated October 1, 1678, is a long and varied one. The first article recorded is "One foure foot chest of drawers seder Sprinkled new, but damnified £1-10.0." Further along are mentioned—

—"one middle size calve skin truncke with drawers. One old leather truncke with lock and key ... one old middle size chest with lock and key. One small old chest with lock and key. Two other old chests without keys and one without hinges."

Quite a number of chests and trunks for one family when it is noted that they had chests of drawers also. When the Rev. Samuel Sewall, so well-known from his voluminous diary, returned from a trip to England in 1689, he brought with him on the ship "America" a trunk for each of his three children, with their names and the dates of their births carved thereon. Presumably these trunks did not come over empty. He brought also a sea-chest, a barrel of books, a large trunk marked H. S. with nails, two smaller trunks, a deal box of linen, a small case of liquors, and a great case of bottles. He slept on a feather bed laid above a straw bed on the voyage, and was comfortably covered with a bedquilt.

American oak was used, however, in many American-made chests. Some of the early chests, particularly those found in the United States, stand flat on the ground. Others have legs, sometimes formed by the continuation of the stiles, as those parts of the chests are called which hold the panels on the sides. The two boards which occupy the top and bottom of the sides and back and front are called the rails. The upper rails in some of the chests of early make have a row of carving on them which adds still further to the beauty of the chest, and in some instances the stiles are also carved. Ordinarily, however, the stiles are plain or with but a slight moulding, and the rails are quite plain. Geometric patterns in arched, diamond, or square form were early employed, each maker copying industriously the patterns used by other makers and only occasionally having the originality to design for himself. After the legs formed by the continuation of the stiles came legs made in the shape of great balls such as were used on much Dutch furniture and were copied by the English makers.

The great Dutch *kas*, or chest, was a very large and ornamental piece of furniture, carved, painted, or decorated in marquetry. Such pieces are unusual now, most of them having been gathered in by collectors or museums, the Dutch towns along the Hudson, as well as Albany and Schenectady, having been pretty well picked over.

The evolution of the bureau from the chest is an interesting study, and shows plainly the different periods through which the useful and homely "kist" passed before it emerged into such an ornamental thing as the carved and decorated highboy. The first step in its upward career was taken when a drawer was added below the chest proper. This came as early as the last half of the seventeenth century, those chests belonging to the first half being without drawers. Sometimes this single drawer was divided, and the very earliest specimens had the runners on which the drawers moved on the sides, and not on the bottom, as came later. The sides of the drawer were hollowed out in a groove, and a stout runner was affixed to the side of the chest. Such a chest is shown. With the appearance of drawers came a difference in ornamentation, and mouldings in great variety were used, beading and turned drops also coming in for use. These patterns were merely the familiar mouldings used in wainscots and panellings put to the purpose of adorning the chests. The early chests without drawers ran in the neighbourhood of five feet long and twenty-four inches high. As the drawers were added, the chests naturally rose in height, and to prevent their becoming too bulky they decreased in length.

A nice example of one of these early oak chests, mounted on turned legs and with curved strainers, is shown. It is in a fine state of preservation and has the original brass escutcheons. It was evidently intended as a receptacle for valuables, as both drawer and chest are made to lock. It belongs to the Waring Galleries, London. Two drawers followed one, the chest portion still retaining its prominence, and in this simple way the chest of drawers grew from the box-like affair of 1600 and later. By 1710 chests were looked upon as "old," and so advertised for sale, although they continued to be made until the middle of the eighteenth century. They were too useful to be abandoned by a people who were obliged to be often on the move, and who needed some stout receptacle in which to carry their household and personal goods.

Turned Chair with Leather Cover

There are chests which are peculiar to certain localities, notably in New England, which were doubtless made by a single cabinet-maker, his workmen and apprentices. They are almost entirely confined to these localities, and are therefore of less interest to the collector in general than such pieces as are more widely distributed. Under this head comes that style of receptacle known as the Hadley Chest, and the Connecticut chest shown in Chapter V. The Dutch chests were often of pine, painted, only the choicest ones being of walnut. One inventory records a "chest brought from Havanna,"—probably Spanish.

After matters became a little less anxious for the early settlers, personal comfort began to be thought of more, and such colonists as had brought no chairs began to send for them to England or have them made in America. Every ship from England took out fresh comforts, and the dignitaries of the colonies had substantial household gear. Tables, chairs, beds, and carpets,—these latter not for floors, but for use as table-covers,—are mentioned with great frequency in the inventories, and the settlers' house, albeit many of them boasted of but four rooms, had more than a modest degree of luxury.

The New Haven Colony—as indeed did all the Colonies—had, as her chief officers, men used to the best that England afforded, and the following inventory speaks for itself. John Haynes, governor of Connecticut, in 1653 left an estate at Hartford valued at £1,400. In his hall, one of the most esteemed parts of the house at this period, were,—

5 leather and 4 flag-bottomed chairs	1 table and 3 joined stools	1 carbine
1 firelock musket	1 matchlock do.	1 gilded looking-glass
1 pr. cob-irons	1 iron back	7 cushions
	1 tin hanging candlestick	1 rapier
		1 smoothing-iron

—the whole valued at £8 13s. 10d. The parlor had velvet chairs and stools, also Turkey-wrought chairs, and a green cloth carpet valued at £1 10s. There were also curtains of say, curtain rods and "vallants," many napkins, as these were necessary from lack of forks, and much Holland bed and table linen. There were many chests and "lean-to" or livery cupboards.

"The men's chamber," had "a bedstead with two flock beds; one feather boulster, one flock do.; one blanket; one coverlet." His best rooms had feather beds. In the cellar were many brewing-vessels and wooden-ware, while the kitchen had a complete "garnish" of pewter, but not a single piece of crockery. Brass candlesticks, iron possnets and porringers, and the useful brass warming-pan were here also. Theophilus Eaton, also governor of Connecticut, left in 1657 an inventory of goods of even greater value.

Even earlier than this, rich furniture was imported by those who could afford it, and in 1645 a Mistress Lake, sister-in-law of Governor Winthrop the younger, sent to England for the furnishings for her daughter's new house. There were many items in the list, and among them were only one—

—"bedsteede of carven oak; 2 armed cheares with fine rushe bottums; three large & three small silvern spoons, & 6 of horne."

As late as 1755 "armed cheares" were highly esteemed, and Joseph Allison, of Albany, N. Y., bequeathed two to his second son, a walking-cane to his firstborn, and to his youngest son some clothes. Chairs, stools, and cushions are mentioned in many inventories as being covered with "set work;" this was heavy woolen tapestry much after the fashion of Oriental rugs, and most durable. It is rather unusual to find no mention of leather chairs in inventories, for they were used in America late in 1600, and chairs covered with "redd lether," as well as with Spanish leather, are of frequent occurrence.

Lion Gardiner was one of the chief proprietors of Easthampton, L. I., in 1653, where he passed the last ten years of his life "rummaging old papers" and in other peaceful pursuits. The inventory of his estate is set out fully and seems scant enough.

2 Great Bookes	Swine	A stubing how
4 Great cheirs	Bedding	A little how
13 peeces of hollow pewter	Cooking utensils	Cattle
	A cheese press	Clothing
5 pewter spoons	several bookes	2 pastry boards
A broad how	15 peeces of pewter	A cickell
Horses	4 porringers & 4 saucers	A churn

It was this same Lion Gardiner who, after the Pequot War, bought from the Indians the island Monchonock, embracing thirty-five acres of hill and dale. The price paid was a large black dog, a gun, some powder and shot, a few Dutch blankets. This is the place which we know to-day as Gardiner's Island. The "great cheirs" mentioned in the inventory were, no doubt, either Turkey-work or leather, and seem to be the only articles of this kind of furniture possessed by him.

In 1638, in London, a man named Christopher took out a patent for decorating leather, which somewhat reduced its cost. Up to this time all leather was imported from Spain or Holland.

English Chair - c. 1680   Italian Chair - Same period

The fine example of a Portuguese or Spanish leather chair, as they were variously called, and shows well the splendid and ornamental leather as well as the rich carving seen particularly on the front brace. The leather is fastened to the frame with large brass nails, and that part of the oak frame which is exposed is turned work. On many of these chairs there are three little metal ornaments on the curved top. In this example two are lost. Besides the carving on the front brace, a pattern which was often adopted and copied by English and Dutch cabinet-makers, this chair shows well that form of foot which came to be known as the "Spanish foot." It is seen on all makes of furniture, and with some variations of form, but

21

always turns out at the base, and has the grooved work so conspicuous. There is no doubt that this was an exceedingly popular style of chair, for there are many examples almost exactly like this in many collections. This particular one is in the Boston Museum of Fine Arts.

Another style of leather chair is shown, and its solidity is a great contrast to the Spanish chair previously shown. The woodwork is turned, and the heavy underbracing shaped, while the second bracing is a feature peculiar to this chair itself. The date of this piece is probably about 1650, or a little later,—about the same date as similar turned pieces which are covered with Turkey work. The leather on the seat is so old and worn that it seems as if it had never been renewed, while the back is much fresher and looks comparatively new. The seat of this chair is so high from the floor that a footstool was a necessity, and in the old inventories the item of "low stools," or "foot-banks" appears with some frequency. This chair is of about the same period as the Spanish leather chairs. Many leather chairs are found in the United States, both North and South, and are probably of English make. Some inventories mention them as "old," as early as 1667, and many were in use in different parts of the country.

Cane Chair, Flemish Style

But while most of our early New England colonists were grappling with the serious business of life, almost content if they could scrape together enough to eat and to wear, and a substantial roof to cover them, in England life was taking a more ornamental aspect. Charles II., indolent and fond of luxury, came to the throne in 1660. Two years later he married Catherine of Braganza, a Portuguese princess, and both of them introduced a more elegant style of living; his French and her Spanish training leading them to require more comforts than had hitherto been known in England.

Among other things which were exported from Holland was cane furniture of a superior quality. It became very much the fashion, and was in Spanish or Flemish styles, both of which were copied or adapted by English cabinet-makers. Some of this furniture found its way to America, and there are pieces to be found showing all three styles, Flemish, Spanish, and English adaptation. An example of the

22

English treatment of the Spanish style, at least as to foot; while the flat underbrace is English, the curved back and bandy leg are quite Dutch. The carving on the top is very beautiful, and the knees of the front legs carved, not with the usual shell, but with heads, and below these an oval with moulding. This chair is in the South Kensington Museum, London, and dates from about 1680. The wood is walnut, and the scrolls and foliage on the back stand out in high relief; the seat, originally as now, is covered with a rich brocade, with fine brass nails and a fringe.

The second chair is one of about the same period, of very beautifully carved oak, and not restored. The arms are missing, but show the places where they originally were. It has lost its feet, but the exquisite carving on the underbrace and top is still quite intact and quite Italian in style. This chair is at the Waring Galleries, London.

A very splendid example of the Flemish treatment of the same style is shown on the previous page, the oak woodwork being carved and turned, and the foot turning out in true Flemish style. The date of the chairs shown in both Figures 8 and 9 is prior to 1700.

The wealthy people of Charles II.'s time all indulged in these chairs. Before that period stools had been in general use, and only the master, mistress, or guest of honour occupied the few chairs possessed in a household.

In New England centres like Salem, Boston, or New Haven, even before the time of Charles II., there was in some of the houses comfort as we understand it. Mr. George Lamberton, of the New Haven Colony, sailed in 1646 to England upon business in the "Great Ship." She was never heard from again, and her loss crippled the little colony almost beyond belief. Mr. Lamberton's inventory shows a variety of items. He had as many as eighty napkins; bedding and table, chimney and board cloths in proportion; feather and down beds with their accompanying hangings. These with more than a dozen cushions to make soft the stiff chairs and settles, silver plate, four chests, ten boxes and trunks, eleven chairs, five stools, and three tables, both round and square, made up comfortable furnishings for a house with probably not more than four rooms. The colonists were not only "plain people," but there were those who came, shortly after the first settlement, who brought with them the household goods and clothes to which they had been accustomed.

23

The "Journal of the Pilgrims at Plymouth" tells not only of the stress of living and the struggle with Indians and forest creatures. There was time to reprehend the frivolities of women's wear, and the pastor's wife was the chief offender in the matter of over-gay apparel. She was a young widow when Mr. Johnson married her, and brought goodly estate and personal belongings to her second husband. She continued to wear the clothes she had brought with her, and the chief exceptions were taken to the cork-soled shoes she wore, and the whalebone in the bodice and sleeves of her gown. Both the pastor and his wife seem to have been more than reasonable, since they were willing to reform the cut of their garments as far as they could "without spoiling of them."

While the general habit of the Puritans was to keep their houses and apparel extremely plain, yet here and there among them bits of comfort and elegance would crop out. Among the stiff and straight-backed chairs, one with stuffing would be found, while in the more luxurious and easy-going South they were not so rare.

The covering probably was "sett work or Turkey work;" but then, too, brocade ones were found, and such a chair as is shown would be an ornament in any home. It is a fine example of walnut-wood, turned and carved with bannister back and stuffed

Turned and Curved Armchair

seat. The covering has been restored, but is of a pattern which was of the period. The out-turned Flemish foot is more ball-like in shape than is often seen, but it has the bowed knees which are so familiar.

Yet, if the chairs were none too comfortable, there were few families in any of the settlements that did not own at least one feather bed. If not feathers, then "flock beds" were used, that is chopped rags, or feathers and flock mixed, or, as a last resort, the down from the brown soft, cat-tails which grew plentifully in every marsh was utilized instead of more costly material.

Dutch Furniture

Probably the first pieces of furniture that were landed on the shores of the Hudson came in the ship *Fortune*, and were brought by Hendrich Christiansen, of Cleep, who founded a little settlement of four houses and thirty persons in 1615. A little later came the *Tiger*, *The Little Fox*, and the *Nightingale*, all bringing colonists and their household furniture. The early Dutch settlers were better fitted to start an infant colony than their New England brothers.

While revered for their elaborate dollhouses, the Dutch nevertheless accomplished much in furniture design. Image: Typezero

The Dutch were ever colonizers and knew just how to plan and prepare a settlement. The trouble with the Indians was not so constant as it was with the New England colonies, although on one occasion New Amsterdam was almost wiped out. On the whole, the Dutch seem to have treated the Indians more wisely, buying the lands of them and having the purchase further confirmed by grants.

In New Amsterdam the settlers were comfortably fixed, comparatively speaking, long before the New England colonists were, for they had a sawmill in operation as early as 1627, the machinery for which had been sent from Holland, and which was worked by wind-power.

The Dutch settled at Albany and its neighbourhood and around Schenectady, as well as those at New Amsterdam, had many creature comforts. In 1643 Albany was a colony of about one hundred persons living in about thirty rough board houses. By 1689 the number of inhabitants had increased to 700 and the houses to 150. During the next ten years the improvements were rapid and wonderful; gardens grew, filled with flowers and fruit; the class of houses improved; wealthy merchants came to such a rich market (of furs chiefly); and the Dutch city grew apace, and the fine beaver-skins which were so plenty bought luxuries for the pioneers.

That luxury is not too strong a word to use is shown by the splendid carved kas shown on the next page, which now belongs to the Albany Historical Society, and is a piece of furniture which may date back as far as the last quarter of the seventeenth century. It is made of walnut, and stands over eight feet high, with cupboard and shelves. While this chest was of unusual beauty, there was a certain solidity and ponderous character observable in most of the Dutch furniture.

Dutch Furniture of the Queen Anne period

It is characteristic of the people themselves and is noted in everything belonging to them. Their very ships had long, high-sounding names, *The Angel Gabriel*, *The Van Rensselaer Arms*, *King David*, *Queen Esther*, *King Solomon*, *The Great Christopher*, *The Crowned Sea-Bears*, and brought in their flat hulks fine goods from all quarters.

The dress of the portly Dutch *vrouw* was in unison with her cleanliness and love of thrift, for her gown—whether of cloth, or her very bettermost one of silk—was cut short enough to well clear the ground, and showed her shoes with shining buckles,

Carved Kas

and her bright-coloured stockings, often clocked with her favorite flower, the tulip. The hair was drawn back from the brow, smoothed and flattened and covered with a cap which, among the wealthy, was bordered with Flanders lace, and in any case was fluted, plaited, and snowy white.

The practical education which the Dutch women always obtained in their own country sharpened their judgment, and the laws which permitted her to hold real estate and carry on business in her own name, even if a married woman, gave her an added independence. It was no unusual thing for women to engage in business on their own account and to carry it on without the aid or interference of the men of the family. At home in the Low Countries, the women had sold at the market, beside the produce of the gardens and poultry yards, the products of their own industry as well,—laces, linen, cloth of wool, etc., and as early as 1656 they sought and obtained permission to hold their market in the new country as they had in the old. Curaçao provided for them many luxuries, such as "lemons, parrots, and paroquettes," besides a variety of liquors. The women grew flax in their own door-yards for the finest linen, and every house had its spinning-wheel.

Hospitality was dispensed at these homes, supper being a favorite meal, and as "early to bed and early to rise" was a national motto the guests were expected to come early and to leave early also,—nine o'clock verging on riotous dissipation. Madam Steenwych was noted for her suppers, which were more substantial than the waffles and tea which was the usual menu. In 1664, after her husband's death, she married Dominie Selyns. At this time she had in her living-room twelve Russia leather chairs, two easy-chairs with silver lace, one cupboard of fine French nut-wood, one round and one square table, one cabinet, thirteen pictures, one dressing-box, cushions, and curtains. Her chairs with silver lace may have well been like the handsome pair of marquetry ones shown in Figure 13. The seat of the side chair is entirely gone, but the arm-chair yet retains a portion of its cover of wool plush, no doubt the original one, since some of the stuffing protrudes, and it is dried sea-kale instead of hair. The wood is maple with an inlay of satin-wood. These chairs belong to the Museum connected with Cooper Institute, New York, which is being carefully gathered by the Misses Hewitt.

Property had become valuable, and loss had been sustained by fire, so in August, 1658, 250 leather fire-buckets for public use were ordered from Holland, together with hooks and ladders. In addition each household was required to have a certain number of buckets of their own, which were to be kept hanging under the back stoop.

In 1686 a rich Dutch burgher in New Amsterdam owned a house of eight rooms over cellars filled, no doubt, with choice liquors and schnapps, and the rooms above set out with chairs and tables, cabinets, cupboards and a "great looking-glass." Ornaments were there, too,—alabaster images and nineteen gaily decorated porcelain dishes. Nor was the house suffered to want for thorough cleansing, as there were thirteen scrubbing and thirty-one rubbing brushes, twenty-four pounds of Spanish soap, and seven other brushes. With an increase of prosperity our Dutch housewives lost no whit of their notions of cleanliness, for here is a housecleaning described, presumably by a victim, a hundred years later.

"The husband gone, the ceremony begins. The walls are stripped of their furniture; paintings, prints, and looking-glasses lie in huddled heaps about the floors; the curtains are torn from their testers, the beds crammed into windows; chairs and tables, bedsteads and cradles crowd the yard; and the garden fence bends beneath the weight of carpets, blankets, cloth cloaks, old coats, under-petticoats, and ragged breeches. This ceremony completed, and the house thoroughly evacuated, the next operation is to smear the walls and ceilings with brushes dipped into a solution of lime called whitewash; to pour buckets of water over the floor and scratch all the partitions and wainscots with hard brushes charged with soft soap and stone-cutter's sand."

Even these thrifty pioneers did not all accrue many goods, for 1707, when Hellegonda De Kay, of New York, came to make her will, she was obliged to leave her "entire worldly estate" to one daughter. It consisted of one Indian slave. The Dutch wife had an equal interest with her husband in disposing of household goods and furniture. She was always consulted, and sometimes she even signed the will with her husband. The wives of the English settlers, whether Quaker or Puritan, did not have the rights of their Dutch sisters in the ownership of household goods. The wife's dowry passed into her husband's hands at marriage, and remained there until his death, as the inventory of the estate of Alexander Allyn of Hartford, Conn., who died in 1708, testifies.

"*Estate that deceased had with his wife Elizabeth in marriage (now left to her).*"

"One round table; bed with furnishings; chest of drawers; two trunks; a box; books; earthenware; glasses; pewter platters; plates; bason; porringers; cups; spoons; tinware; a fork; trenchers; four chairs; nine pounds in silver money; table-cloths; napkins; towels; a looking-glass; a chest; a silver salt; porringer; wine-cup and spoon; a brass pot; an iron pot; two brass skillets and hooks."

The following extract from a will drawn in 1759 by a man eighty years old shows the Friend's point of view as to whom the household stuff belonged. He wills to his wife as long as she liveth, unless she marries again (she was seventy years old at the time),

"two good feather beds and full furniture, and all my negro bedding; and all my grain, either growing or cut, or in store at the time of my decease; and all my flax and wool, and yarn and new cloth and cattle hides, leather, and soap, and meat, and all other provisions which I have in store in my house, either meat or drink, and all my negro men and one of my negro women, such of them as she shall choose, and my negro girl named Priss; and if I should chance to dye when I have cattle a-fatting my wife shall have them for the provision of herself and family, at my wife's disposal."

No doubt the feather beds and "negro bedding," as well as the "new cloth," had been made by the patient fingers of this wife of fifty years' standing; but she must forfeit all this fruit of her labour should she marry again. The Dutch system seems preferable.

In another inventory, that of Charles Mott, also a Long Island Quaker, dated 1740, the eldest son has the house and homestead, "together with the negro boy Jack and one feather bed." The sole provision for his wife was "four pounds a year" to be paid to her by the eldest son "so long as she remains my widow." He seems to have put a premium on her filling his place, and that quickly.

Possibly our Dutch settlers were more notable house wives than their sisters in New England or the South. In the latter region the mistress did not contribute with her own hands to the cleanliness of her home, but she had onerous duties in overlooking the work of sometimes over a hundred negroes, seeing to their food, clothes, and shelter. Our New England wives were still suffering from Indian depredations, and the young housewives whose doors were driven thick with nails to repel the deadly tomahawk, as Mistress David Chapin's was at Chicopee in 1705, would probably not have risked her "goods" out of doors, as did the Dutch housewives at Albany.

The Dutch kitchen utensils seem numerous and varied. Possets, pans, jack-spits, strainers and skillets were seen in inventories as well as the more familiar pots and kettles. The prosperous Dutch at home had sent

Marquetry Chairs

out and brought back many a rich argosy, and silks and tissues, porcelains and lacquers, carved ivory and fantastic carved wood, spices and plants had been brought to Holland and found their way to America. There were many ships unloaded at New York filled with spoils from the East, which were eagerly bought up. There was a variety of moneys current,—beaver-skins; wampum; Spanish pistoles, worth 17s. 6d.; Arabian chequins at 10s.; "pieces of eight" (as the Spanish reals were called), which, if they weighed 16 pennyweight (except those of Peru) passed for 5s.; and French crowns worth 5s. Peruvian pieces of eight and Dutch dollars were valued at 4s., and all English coin passed "as it goes in England." These were the values in 1705, but they varied somewhat, the currency being inflated by one governor, though his act created such a disturbance that he was obliged to withdraw it. The Long Island Dutch seem to have had less rich belongings than those up the Hudson and about Albany. Around Jamaica and Hempstead were stout clapboard and shingle houses, but the inventories are not lavish. Daniel Denton, writing in 1670 "A Brief Description of New York," says this about his dearly loved Hempstead.

"May you should see the woods and Fields so curiously bedeckt with Roses and an innumerable multitude of delightful Flowers not only pleasing to the eye but smell. That you may behold Nature contending with Art and striving to equal if not excel many gardens in England."

But he has little to say about the way of living, except that it is "godly."

The records of New Amsterdam, which are so wonderfully complete, show what a valuable assistant to these first settlers was the powerful West India Company. By 1633 there were five stone houses containing the Company's workshops; and as the land near at hand was poor,—"scrubby" the Dutch farmers called it,—they spread out to the neighbouring New Jersey, Long Island, Gowanus, and East River shores and from 1636 to 1640 were busy with their settlements.

By 1651 New Amsterdam was prosperous enough to have a brick house so good and well-built as to be worth 5,195 florins (about $2,100 of our money). In 1649 Adam Roelantsen, a general factotum of the West India Company, whose name constantly appears in the town records, (as he was unfortunately addicted to strong waters, and under these conditions was very quarrelsome and aggressive,) owned the following house. It was a clapboard structure covered with a reed roof, and eighteen by thirty feet in size. It stood gable end toward the street, and at the front door was the usual "portal" with its wooden seats. Outside of the frame the chimney of squared timber was carried up, while within the fireplace had a mantelpiece and the living room had "fifty-one leaves of wainscot." There was a bedstead or state-bed built in, but of the movables no record is left. In reading these old records it is noticed that matters moved quickly; not much time was spent in grief and repining; and to illustrate we give the experience of one woman whose career does not seem to have excited any comment among her contemporaries. In 1685 William Cox married a young woman named Sarah Bradley, who had come from England with her father and brothers to settle in New Amsterdam. She was said to have been handsome and dashing, and certainly she needed spirit to carry her through her subsequent career. Four years after her marriage her husband met with the following accident, thus described by a political opponent.

"Mr. Cox, to show his fine clothes, undertook to goe to Amboy to proclaime the King, who, coming whome againe, was fairely drowned, which accident startled our commanders here very much; there is a good rich widdow left. The manner of his being drowned was comeing on board a cannow from Capt Cornelis' Point at Staten Islands, goeing into the boate, slipt down betwixt the cannow and the boate, the water not being above his chin, but very muddy, stuck fast in, and, striving to get out, bobbing his head under, receaved to much water in. They brought him ashore with life in him, but all would not fetch him againe."

The good rich "widdow" whom he left soon changed her loneliness for the pleasures of married life, this time with Mr. John Oort. He, too, made a brief stay, for by May 16, 1691, the widow Sarah Oort had the necessary license under colonial law for her marriage to no less a person than Captain William Kidd. They lived comfortably in a house left by Sarah's first husband, Mr. Cox (who left her with an estate of several thousand pounds) till Captain Kidd set out on his notable voyage in the "Adventure."

The goods which Mrs. Oort had at the time of her marriage to Captain Kidd were the following: fifty-four chairs, of Turkey work and double and single nailed; five tables with their carpets (covers); four curtained beds with their outfits; three chests of drawers; two dressing-boxes; a desk; four looking-glasses; two stands; a screen; a clock; andirons; fire-irons; fenders; chafing-dishes; (3) candlesticks of silver, brass, pewter, and tin; leather fire-buckets; over one hundred ounces of silver plate; and a dozen glasses. The screen, no doubt, was such a one as is shown in the same figure, No. 14, as the Dutch cradle, which was used for many years in the Pruyn family, of Albany. The third object in the picture is what is known as a church stool, and was useful in keeping the good *vrouw's* feet off the cold floors. This stool is painted black and is dated 1702. There is a lurid picture of the Last Judgment painted on it, and also a verse in Dutch, which reads as follows:

"The judgment of God is now at hand. There is still time; let us separate the pious from the wicked and entreat God for the joy of heaven."

All these articles are now at the rooms of the Historical Society, Albany.

William Kidd was executed in May, 1701, and, nothing daunted by her matrimonial ventures, Sarah took as her fourth husband, in 1703, Christopher Rousby, a man of considerable influence in the colony. She lived until 1745, and left surviving her four children.

While the houses were rough, some with but two rooms, yet articles even of luxury were there and offered for sale. As early as 1654 a casket inlaid with ebony was sold and brought thirty beavers and nineteen guilders. Cornelis Barentsen sued Cristina Capoens in 1656 for payment for a bed he sold her, payment to be made in fourteen days. The price was six beavers (about $57.00), which Cristina seemed unable to pay, but which payment was ordered by the court. In June, 1666, the administrators of the estate of the late Jan Ryerson sold some "beasts" (horses, calves, and hogs), as well as furniture at public sale. "The payment for the beasts, also the bed, bolsters, and pillows," was to be made in "whole merchantable beavers, or otherwise in good strung seewant, beavers' price, at twenty-four guilders the beaver."

Here is the inventory of a bride who was married at New Amsterdam in 1691, and although her husband was a man of consideration and some wealth it was deemed of sufficient importance to record.

"A half-worn bed; one pillow; two cushions of ticking, with feathers; one rug; four sheets; four cushion-covers; two iron pots; three pewter dishes; one pewter basin; one iron roster; one schuryn spoon; two cowes about five years old; one case or cupboard, one table."

August 31, 1694, Jan Becker's inventory entered at Albany, New York, showed a long list. Besides abundant household goods he had—

"A silver spoon; 3 pr. gold buttons; 5 doz. & 10 silver buttons for shirts; & 2 silver scnuffies."

It is not difficult to picture in the mind how these old Dutch houses looked when the living-room was made snug and warm of a winter's evening. At various places along the Hudson and on Long Island there are still standing some of these old, low-ceiled, wooden houses, with sloping roof and great chimney. The furniture was generally of oak (particularly if it had been brought from home) and carved. The most important objects in the room are the mantelpiece and the bed, the former of

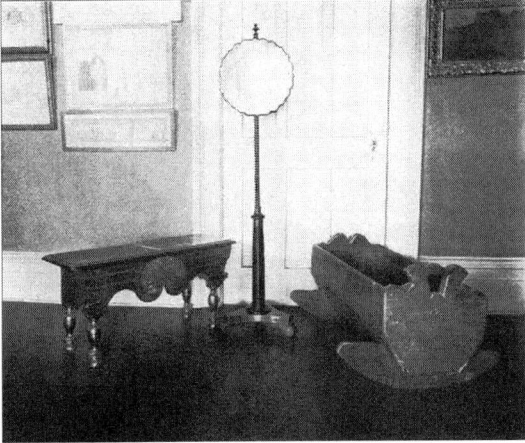

Dutch Screen, Cradle and Church Stool

carved wood, its ornate character significant of the wealth of the owner, and its size seldom less than the height of the room. The bed was frequently built in the room, a sort of bunk, hung with curtains often of bright chintz, though, judging from the inventories, "purple calico" curtains were immensely popular, just as this same fabric is beloved to-day by the pretty maid-servants one sees tripping through the quaint old streets of Holland. There were stools; not many chairs; tables, one or two; each with its bright carpet or cover; racks on the wall for what delft the mistress had; and below it the treasured spoons. In the great kas, which took up a large portion of the room, was the linen, covers for tables, side-tables, shelves, etc., and all the napkins and choice belongings of the housewife. If this kas was carved oak it sometimes stood on a frame; sometimes it had ponderous locks. If it was painted or inlaid wood it might reach nearly to the floor, and then stand upon large ball feet. Some of these kas were so large and heavy that it was almost impossible to move them, and there is the record of one *vrouw* who upon moving from Flatbush was obliged to abandon hers, leaving it behind her and selling it for £25:

In the Van Rensselaer family is a marriage kas which goes back to the beginning of the eighteenth century. It was imported from Holland by the parents of Katherine Van Brugh, who wished their only daughter to have everything that money could buy, and during her early years it was being filled with linen and household goods woven under her father's roof. It was no light task to fill this great chest, for it stood seven feet high and proportionally wide. It is of carved oak, has

32

many drawers and receptacles, and will hold the silver and finery of the mistress, while there are secret drawers for "duccatoons and jacobuses." The keyhole is concealed under a movable cover of carved wood, which looks like a part of the carving when dropped in place. The ponderous key is of iron and has many wards.

If the family was quite well to do and owned a good stock of clothes, there would be one or more smaller cases, or chests, in which these were stored away. Much furniture was made here by Dutch workmen, who followed the fashions of their native land. They found abundant material, and more was brought into the country,—in devious ways sometimes, but still it came.

The court records for New Amsterdam for 1644 report a bark, *Croisie*, of Biscay, which was brought into the harbour as a prize by the ship *La Garce*, being laden with sugar, tobacco, and ebony. The claim of the master of the *La Garce* was granted, and the goods sold.

Nearly always there was a little silver,—spoons, mugs, and a salt-cellar; and, as years passed on, much coin was beaten by some member of the family (for there were many Dutch silversmiths) into tankards,—splendid heavy vessels, capable of holding a quart, with cover and thumb-piece, and showing the marks of the mallet on the bottom and inside, for all of these pieces of plate were hand-made. Waiters and massive bowls were seen in nearly every family of easy circumstances, and they scarcely ever went out of the family, as it was a matter of pride to retain them. Much of this fine old plate is treasured to-day by descendants of its former owners. It has survived better than the furniture, indestructible as that seemed.

In 1739 Lowrens Claesen, of Schenectady, had, among other property, a gold seal ring and a silver cup marked "L. V. V." Myndert Fredricksen of Albany County, New York, blacksmith, left in 1703 a great silver tankard, a church book with silver clasps and chains, and a silver tumbler marked "M. F." A blacksmith in those days meant a worker in iron, and this one must have been prosperous, for he owned his house and land, and furniture as well as silver.

But even if silver were lacking there were brass skillets and warming-pans, and pewter was the ordinary table furniture, which was scoured to a polish little short of silver. One or two pieces of brightly decorated Delft ware was the crowning glory of the housewife's treasures, and far too precious for every-day use. So holes were drilled in the edge, and a stout cord passed through, so that it could be hung upon the wall. There was, of course, a clock also, and leather chairs. Nicholas Van Rensselaer, of Albany, who died in 1679, was a wealthy and important member of the colony of Albany.

His house had two beds, two looking-glasses, two chests of drawers, two tables, one of oak and one of nut-wood; also a table of pine, as well as six stools of the same; a sleeping-bunk or built-in bed, over twenty pictures, a desk, and, of course, brushes and kitchen utensils. These goods were disposed of through four rooms. Not only were all the necessaries abundant, but some very elegant furniture came in with almost every ship, and even before 1700, ebony chairs, boxes and cabinets are mentioned in the inventories; but such splendid pieces as the cabinet pictured, with carved panels in the doors, and carved twisted legs, were only occasionally to be met with. The doors conceal shelves, and above are two drawers with drop handles. There are pieces similar to this to be found in the United States in private houses as well as in museums. This cabinet belongs to the Waring Galleries, London.

Children slept in trundle beds, which during the day were pushed under the large bed, often a four-post bedstead when not the sleeping-bunk. One thing was found in every house, rich or poor, and this was some means for striking fire. Tinder and steel, with scorched linen, were an indispensable part of every household. Sometimes it was necessary to borrow coals from a neighbour, and there were stringent town laws ordering that "fire shall always be covered when carried from house to house." In the "Court Records of New Amsterdam" one of the earliest laws regulated the carrying about of hot coals, and several Dutch *vrouws* were hauled to court for breaking them.

Ebony Cabinet

The furniture in these houses was by no means all of Dutch or domestic make. They had what they were able to get, and among painted kas and inlaid chests would be Spanish chairs or stools, and English walnut beds with serge hangings, folding tables and Turkey-work chairs. Before the close of the seventeenth century there came direct to New York Dutch ships from the Orient, or from the Low Countries themselves, loaded with rich goods, among which was much furniture. Styles had begun to change a little; the Dutch were absorbing ideas from the Chinese and copying and adapting forms and decorations. Beautiful lacquer work was coming in, and splendid inlaid or marquetry work; not any more in two colours, as was the earliest style, but in a variety of colours and in divers patterns, and standing upon bandy legs with ball and claw, or what is known as the Dutch foot, instead of the straight or turned leg.

The inventories show how far East Indian goods were coming in, and there is frequent mention of "East India baskets," boxes, trunks, and even cabinets. The most usual woods were black walnut, white oak and nut-wood, which was hickory. Occasionally pieces were made of olive-wood, or of pine-wood painted black. Ebony was used for inlay and for adornment for frames. Looking-glasses were mentioned in nearly every list, the earliest coming from Venice. By 1670 looking-glass was manufactured at Lambeth, England, in the Duke of Buckingham's works, and was not now so costly as to be seen only among the wealthy. The cupboards were no longer uniformly made with solid doors, but glass was introduced, so that the family wealth of silver and china could be easily seen. By 1727 mahogany is mentioned occasionally in the inventories, and it could be bought by those who were wealthy enough to afford it.

Probably the Spaniards were the earliest users of mahogany, followed by the Dutch and English. Furniture made of this wood is known to have existed in New York prior to 1700, and in Philadelphia a little later. The old Spanish mahogany was a rich, dark, heavy wood, susceptible of a high polish. It darkened with age and was not stained. The new mahogany, at least that which comes from Mexico, is of a light, more yellow colour, and requires staining, as age does not darken it. It is light in weight. The mere lifting of a piece enables one to judge whether it is made from Spanish wood.

The carpets referred to in nearly every inventory were not floor-coverings, but table-covers,—small rugs, no doubt, but far too precious to be worn out by rough-shod feet walking over them. The floors were scoured white, and were strewn with sand which showed the artistic capacity of mistress or maid in the way it had patterns drawn in it by broom-handle or pointed stick. It was not until the middle of the century that carpets became at all common, and even then they are mentioned in the inventories as very choice possessions. There were "flowered carpets," "Scotch ditto," "rich and beautiful Turkey carpets," and Persian carpets also. The colonists traded with Hamburg and Holland for "duck, checquered linen, oznaburgs, cordage, and tea,"—goods appreciated by the housewife, and which she could not make.

The festivities indulged in by the Dutch settlers were generally connected with the table; they played backgammon, or bowls when the weather was fine and they could go out of doors. The cards they used numbered seventy-three to the pack, and

Bed Chair

there was no queen, her place being supplied by a cavalier who was attended by a hired man, and they both supported the king. Cards were not popular, however, except among the English settlers, and they followed the home fashions.

After English rule had been dominant in the little city of New Amsterdam for nearly fifty years the larger number of the families was still Dutch, as a collection of wills made at that period testifies. What would be now domains worthy a prince—farms lying in Nassau Island, as Long Island was then called, vast tracts in New Jersey, and thousands of acres between New York and Albany—were divided by these wills. Such names as Killian Van Rensselaer, second lord of the manor;

35

Harmanus Rutgers, Philip Schuyler, Van Cortlandt, Provoost, etc., are signed to these documents but it is in the minor wills that we find the records of the lives of the main body of the people. A feather bed, one or more slaves, and the family Bible are the bequests usually first specified, the Bibles in some cases being very massive and ponderous affairs. Jarminaye Sieurs, widow, 1709, bequeaths to her daughter her Bible with silver clasps, in addition to her gold rings and one half of her clothes. A grand-daughter, Hilley Veghten, gets a "silver cup with two ears," and other grandchildren, bearing such interesting names as Reynier, Simesse, and Gretie Veghten, get a silver spoon each. In 1711 a fond mother leaves to her daughter "the red and white worsted and linen stockings," besides two pillows, two coverlids, a bed and furniture.

A Hempstead yeoman is very careful to stipulate that his daughter shall have—

"one feather bed, an iron pot, six plates, three platters, two basins, one drinking pot and one cupboard worth £3, and six chairs, six sheep, and one table."

The price of the cupboard being specified shows that it was held in great estimation, and it must have been a handsome piece of furniture.

Only very occasionally do we find a record in the inventories of a "bed chair," yet such were sometimes found here early in the eighteenth century. One is pictured on the previous page. It is carved on the top and inlaid, and covered with woollen plush,—not the original covering, which no doubt was Turkey work. Two hinges are shown on the front rail; the back lets down, and a leg unfolds to

Marquetry Desk

support it; while the legs and arms coming together make the centre firm. This unusual piece is at the Museum connected with the Cooper Institute, is of nut-wood or maple inlaid with tulip-wood, with bandy legs and the well-known Dutch feet.

The Dutch settlers had other elegances which are more rarely met with, such as walnut kas or chests, inlaid with plaques, or rather small saucers and plates of Oriental china. These were tall, with doors opening their whole length, and stood on the great ball feet which are so familiar. One such cabinet is in the Metropolitan Museum, New York. In the former example the plaques display flowers and birds in various colours; in the latter are plain blue and white.

Of later manufacture were pieces of rich marquetry in vari-coloured exotic woods upon mahogany. The heavy foot was replaced by others, still turning out, to be sure, in the Flemish fashion, but very ornate and beautiful, and still further embellished with ornaments in gilt. Such a piece, massive in shape, but enriched with much ornament, is shown in the desk depicted. It was never made for any of the humbler houses of the Dutch settlers, but such a piece was worthy to stand in the study of a wealthy patroon or to belong to some "lord of the manor."

Chippendale Furnishings

IN studying the various periods into which different makes of furniture may be divided, the accentuating of one point, say of ornaments or the structural peculiarities, is noted, not as being sharply defined, but as being a gradual growth. Chippendale did not originate at first. Indeed, he hardly adapted, for the East India trade had brought to market Chinese designs which he used, and French furniture was so popular that he copied bodily in his book such designs as pleased him, although the term "French chairs," as employed at this time, referred to their being upholstered and not to the style or decoration.

A classic folding Pembroke table by Thomas Chippendale - Image: Rauantiques

Thomas Johnson published a book about the middle of the eighteenth century, in which was a medley of French, Gothic and Chinese designs, many of which have a strong family likeness to Chippendale's. There was also Matthias Lock, who began to publish his books as early as 1740, dedicated to such "nobility as would stand for him." These books included one on Pier Frames, Girandoles, Tables, etc., also, one on Ornaments and Sconces, all of which were characteristic of what was considered desirable at this time, and which style Chippendale followed too. Ince & Mayhew published what they called a "Universal System of Household Furnishing."

They made many designs, over three hundred, and not only set forth the fine taste in which they were conceived, but gave the workmen directions for executing them. They positively ran wild on "Chinese taste," their fretwork and combination of Chinese and Gothic being perfectly extravagant. Like Chippendale they designed terms, or as we should call them pedestals, for busts, toilet-tables, bookcases, many mirror-frames, and chairs most intricate in their carved backs, with ribbon-work, scrolls, and elaborate patterns in brass nails.

What were known as "overdoors" were very carefully designed by Chippendale, Ince & Mayhew, Robert Manwaring, and later by the Adam Brothers. These overdoors were the wood or leadwork into which glass was set, to go above front doors.

William Halfpenny, carpenter and architect, as he called himself, published many works on Furniture, Temples, Garden Seats, Windows, Doors, Obelisks, etc., beginning in 1719. Among the many books are these two, "Twenty New Designs of Chinese Lattice and Other Works for Staircases, Gates, Failings, etc.," and also, "Chinese and Gothic Architecture." So fond were the Halfpennys (for the son was later associated with the father) of Chinese work that they seldom missed an opportunity of putting in a Chinese figure. On their ceilings, above the chimney-pieces—

Kitchen, Wayside Inn in Sudbury, Mass

everywhere that decoration could be crowded in,—one is apt to find a Chinese mandarin with pigtail and umbrella.

The originality of Chippendale soon spoke for itself. He worked in so many styles, and has so grown in estimation, that his name is made to cover the greatest variety of designs. When he first came before the public his work met with much adverse criticism. Isaac Ware, a contemporary, writes of him thus:

"It is our misfortune at this time to see an unmeaning scrawl of C's inverted and looped together, taking the place of Greek and Roman elegance even in our most expensive decorations."

But the early extravagances of his designs were soon modified, and even they were touched with a grace which made them pleasing to the eye while wholly extravagant. His better and more familiar work is to-day the model upon which cabinet-workers rely, no one having arisen who can improve on his designs. Thousands of pieces of furniture are called by his name, both in this country and England, which were not even contemporary with this maker and bear no resemblance either to his designs or to work known to be his.

About the time that Chippendale came on the field (1750) it had become the custom for architects and designers to publish catalogues of their designs. Thomas Chippendale, a progressive business man, was not behind his contemporaries, so in 1754 he published his catalogue, which he called "The Gentleman's and Cabinet-Maker's Director." It was a very successful publication, passed through several editions, and brought him added name and fame. It sold for £3 13s. 6d., and had fine copper-plate engravings. The title page of Chippendale's "Director," specifies designs for the following pieces of furniture:

"Chairs, Sofas, Beds and Couches, China-Tables, Bason-Tables and Tea-Kettle Stands, Frames for Marble Slabs, Bureau-Dressing-Tables, and Library-Tables, Library Bookcases, Organ Cases for Private Rooms or Churches, Desks and Bookcases, Dressing and Writing-Tables with Bookcases, Toilets, Cabinets, and Clothes-Presses.

China-Cases, China-Shelves, and Book-Shelves, Candle-Stands and Terms for Busts, Stands for China Jars and Pedestals, Cisterns for Water, Lanthorns, and Chandeliers, Fire-Screens, Brackets and Clock-Cases, Pier-Glasses and Table-Frames, Girandoles Chimney-Pieces and Picture-Frames, Stove-Grates, Boarders, Frets, Chinese-Railing and Brass-Work for Furniture."

At this period the best room or "saloon" was wainscotted chair high, and the remainder prepared for wall-paper, or battened for hangings of silk or tapestry. Chippendale drew many beautiful designs, which he calls "borders for paper-hangings," and which were used as finishings at the top of the paper. Some of them were also employed as patterns for carving, or work in stucco painted and gilded.

It must be remembered that Chippendale was par excellence a carver of wood, and so

Chippendale Chairs

we find him working almost exclusively in "solid mahogany," as we have come to call it, which wood had been introduced into England about the time of Raleigh (1595), though it was not used to any extent as a material for furniture until about twenty-five years before Chippendale published his book. Indeed it seems to have been used in America for this purpose quite as soon as in England, although there are in that country a few detached pieces of mahogany furniture made late in 1600, showing that some wood had been imported before Raleigh caused it to be brought in more freely, along with "tabac" and the potato, which latter vegetable was first grown at Sir Walter's estate called "Youghal," near Cork, Ireland. Sir Walter did not use the new wood in his own beautiful house, but had splendidly carved oak chimney-pieces and furniture made by men whom he brought from Flanders for that purpose.

At the time Chippendale published his book he was about forty years old, as it is generally supposed that he was born about 1710. Worcester is given as the place of his birth, and authorities state that other members of his family practiced the art of wood-carving before him, but the information about his early history is very scant. His shop was in St. Martin's Lane, London, and he employed as many as a hundred men, so it is rather strange that more authentic specimens of his handiwork have not survived. While mahogany was the wood which he used chiefly for his furniture, he employed a close-set pine for carving many of the beautiful floriated mirror-frames for which he was so justly celebrated. Scrolls, flower and leaves, falling water, and a particular bird of his own fancy, with a long and prominent beak, were employed in the decoration of these mirrors, which were richly gilded, the ornament being entirely of wood without the addition of porcelain plaques or metal work, which was such a feature of the French furniture of this period, the influence of which is noticeable in many of Chippendale's

designs. It is true that he did not carry out some of his designs, notably such pieces as the state beds, etc., after the style of Louis XV. One glance at the "Director" will show how impossible these beds were. The top, supported on posts, rises like Ossa upon Pelion piled, with layers or terraces of carved figures of children, rock-work, and everything else, the whole crowned by groups consisting of several figures and animals.

His designs for bedposts show the French influence, being fluted and wreathed with flowers. Many stand flat on the ground without ornamental feet, and are plain on top to support a canopy or tester.

Most successful of all the furniture designed by this maker are the chairs, many of them decorated with graceful scroll-work and delicate garlands of flowers, though the styles with which we are most

Chippendale Chair

familiar are massive, heavy pieces with carving upon them, and either with or without solid underbraces. A unique piece is shown in the image. This chair is thought to have been imported into this country about 1760, but I should suppose it to be a very much earlier example of Chippendale's work, while he was still content to copy, for the front legs show the bear's paw while the rear ones are the familiar Dutch foot.

It belongs to the South Carolina College, at Columbia, S. C. and was given to it by General Preston about 1850. In his letter of presentation he calls it "the quasi throne of the Colonial Governors of South Carolina," but beyond this its history is unknown. This chair is of solid mahogany as most of these chairs were, and shows

41

about the edges of the carving traces of the chisel-marks, a not at all unusual feature in these old hand-carved pieces. The splat (*i. e.* the central part of the back) is plainly pierced. The term "cabriole", which we apply now to the leg, in Chippendale's time referred to a chair having a stuffed back. It has generally been supposed that Chippendale was the originator of the ball-and-claw foot, which is of two varieties, but he copied this style of decoration directly from the Dutch. The foot in this chair is what is known as the "bear's paw", so called from the fur which is rudely carved above the foot. The other style being the "bird's claw." The chairs with cabriole legs were called bandy or bow-legged when they first came into use, about 1700, which is also about the time that easy-chairs were first used in bedrooms. Up to that date chairs had been rather severe and of the nature of stools and settles. As writing became better learned there was a demand for dainty and ornamental desks for ladies' use, as well as library desks for men, and bookcases were also needed.

In Chippendale's book, "The Gentleman's and Cabinet-Maker's Director", while there are designs given for every imaginable piece of furniture, there is not a single illustration of the ball-and-claw or hoof foot; yet it is known by authentic pieces, coming down as late as 1780, and preserved in the South Kensington Museum, London, that such work was done by him. Further than this, we are used to consider mahogany as pre-eminently the wood he worked in, yet in this same guide this wood is mentioned by him but once.

"Six designs of chairs for Halls, Passages, or Summer-houses. They may be made either of mahogany or any other wood, and painted, and have commonly wooden seats."

All this fine solid mahogany furniture made by Chippendale, and by which his name is so firmly perpetuated, was regarded by him as merely commercial work. What he really took a pride in was very fussy, covered with upholstery, with an abundance of carving and gilding, and even metal work on the exposed parts. Rosewood was used by him also, with elaborate carving which was sometimes embellished with gilt, or, in cases where great elegance was demanded, by brass, copper, or silver mounts richly chased. He turned out many pieces of soft wood japanned or painted, and decorated also with gilt and colours.

Little of this furniture ever came to America. It was made to order for the nobility and gentry, and its immense cost rendered it possible only for the very wealthy. Among the two hundred copper-plate designs given in Chippendale's book, quite a large portion of them are in what is known as "Chinese taste," which had taken the world of fashion by storm. Sir William Chambers, who had travelled in China, is given the credit for having introduced this style into furniture and decoration, which was further adapted by Chippendale and other makers, but it was already known before Chambers's day. Both Chambers and Robert Adam, the best architects of their day, were Scotchmen. Chambers was born in 1726, and from his earliest years had a love for the sea. This induced him to make a voyage to Canton, where he made innumerable notes and sketches of furniture, buildings, and gardens, which he made full use of later. In 1759 he published his book "The Decorative Part of Civil Architecture," which was most successful. He was appointed drawing-master to the Prince of Wales, afterward George III., and managed to retain the royal favor for the rest of his life. He not only designed many houses for wealthy patrons and altered many others, but he was afterward appointed landscape gardener at Kew, and knighted.

The older Chinese furniture which one sees in Europe dates from the eighteenth century, and was made for and imported by the Dutch; hence the medley of styles. Elaborate bedsteads, tables, and cabinets were decorated with ivory figures in relief. There is furniture of this description in the United States, splendidly carved out of cedar and decorated with hundreds of tiny figures of men and women carved from ivory and set on. Such a piece is pictured, the original of which is at Memorial Hall, Philadelphia.

Carved Cedar Table

Not only was Chinese furniture in wood and wicker brought from the Orient, but the Dutch, whom we have come to look upon as ready imitators, followed Oriental styles not only in furniture but in pottery as well. Chippendale specifies nine of his designs for chairs in Chinese style as proper for a lady's dressing-room, especially if it were hung with an India paper. They were likewise recommended for Chinese temples. These chairs commonly have cane bottoms with loose cushions, but if required may be stuffed and have brass nails.

As early as 1711 Addison comments on the motley confusion heaped up in a lady's library, where there were few books but "Munkies, Mandarins, and Scaramouches" without end; and to keep these ornaments in countenance was also furniture made after Chinese designs.

Besides these styles Chippendale also used a modification of the Gothic, notably in such places as the doors of cabinets, or the doors and the tops of bookcases. Horace Walpole, in his little Gothic villa at Strawberry Hill, had awakened a still further taste for a revival of Gothic designs; and everybody, to be in the mode, had their cabinet doors and bookcases with embattled tops and Gothic tracery. Of all the styles Chippendale adopted and adapted, this one left the least enduring trace. More successful were his bookcases based on Louis XV. style. They are of mahogany and have the rococo ornaments peculiar to this style. This work shows off gilding admirably. These bookcases with drawers and desk, as well

43

as the bureaus, were used in bedrooms which were often boudoirs and studies as well. So a receptacle which could be quickly locked was quite necessary.

In Chippendale's catalogue are directions given for many small articles which were much in demand and highly fashionable when the book was written, but for which the present day and generation has no use. Such were the charming little tea-caddies with brass handles and locks, stands for candles, or china jars or animals with which the drawing-rooms of those days were crowded. There were also carved brackets, decorated with the bird we have spoken of before, and exquisite foliated designs making graceful adornments for any room, and often neglected in sales where other and better-known examples of this period bring fabulous prices. When carved in pine these brackets are always gilded, but occasionally they may be obtained in walnut and mahogany.

The designs for such pieces are largely original with Chippendale, for their use had just become needed, and we must remember besides that it was Chippendale's misfortune to live in a transition period, and that the rococo which preceded him, and by which his first work was influenced, died very hard. Indeed his first style might be called rococo, and the designs swelled and bulged, were covered with meaningless and fantastic ornament, and ran riot through all styles and countries. It had for its chief merit the fact that it was executed with great delicacy and beauty and had a grace about it which was always pleasing. The two sides of a design are seldom alike, and the merit of such pieces is due purely to the skill of the carver. Yet it was under his skilful hand that later the beauty of simplicity was once more proved, and he sought classic models for his inspiration. Speaking himself of designs for French chairs he says, "for greater variety the feet and elbows are different." The moulding around the bottom of the edge of the rails also comes under his consideration, and he mentions Spanish leather or damask as good material for covering chairs.

Chippendale Chairs

He it was who exemplified the principle that each part of a piece of furniture should be adapted to its use, and that overloading an article with ornament did not necessarily add to its beauty. After his rococo period came the rage for Chinese designs, and lastly the plain and solid style with which we are familiar.

Two very handsome chairs are shown in Figure 22, the side chair showing an abundance of exquisite carving on the knees and in the splat. It is wonderful what variety he encompassed working in the small space and confined shape of this part of a chair. It will be observed that in all the chairs shown no two splats are alike.

All the construction of the Chippendale furniture of the last period is remarkably solid and of the first order, and the wood is of a dark and rich mahogany. The best pieces of this period are those in which the originality of the designer had full play, and when he was not influenced by either the French or Oriental taste. The furniture of this period, fine and free in design, was well adapted to the fashions and mode of life of the people for whom it was made. He retained the roomy character of the Dutch furniture, which was needed for the style of dress affected by both sexes. The Spanish furniture of oak, with cane work or leather, introduced by Catherine of Braganza, was not the only innovation brought to England by that lady, for Evelyn says in his "Diary" for May 30, 1662,

"The Queene ariv'd with a traine of Portuguese ladies in their monstrous fardingals or guard-infantas ... Her Majesty in the same habit, her foretop long and curiously turn'd aside."

In the next forty years fashions changed,—they changed slowly in those days,—and among other things laid at the door of "Good Queen Anne" may be added the hoop-skirt. Flowered and damask gowns were worn over it, and in the "Spectator" of 1712 a number of gowns are advertised for sale, all the property of Mr. Peter Paggen, of Love Lane, near Eastcheap, London. Among them is an "Isabella-coloured kincob gown, flowered with green and gold; a purple and gold Atlas gown with a scarlet and gold Atlas petticoat edged with silver."

A little later in the century a lady's gown was all ruffles and flounces, in fact "every part of the garment was in curl, and caused a lady of fashion to look like one of those animals which in the country we call a Friesland hen."

The reigns of the first two Georges had Hogarth for their illustrator, and in the set of drawings called "Marriage à la Mode" we see the hoods, skirts without trains, unruffled and often accompanied by a sack, or something between a cloak and a gown, and called a mantua. During the reign of George I. there was no queen to set the fashion, so it changed little. In 1735 Caroline, queen of George II. on the king's birthday appeared in a "beautiful suit made of silk of the produce of Georgia, and the same was acknowledged to excel that of any other country." The ladies who accompanied her wore flowered silks of various colours, of a large pattern, but mostly with a white ground, with wide short sleeves and short petticoats. These gowns were often pinned up behind in fantastic fashion, and generally quite narrow. It was also à la mode to wear gold or silver nets on the petticoats, and to face and guard the robes with them and even to wear them on sleeves. Lady Harcourt, a famous beauty of Caroline's court, wore on one occasion a "white ground rich silk, embossed with gold and silver, and fine coloured flowers of a large pattern."

What we know as a morning-gown they called, in the middle of the eighteenth century a nightgown, and we read of a "garnet-coloured lustring nightgown with a

45

tobine stripe of green and white, trimmed with floss of the same colour and lined with straw-coloured lutestring." A gay garment truly.

These were the styles in vogue when Chippendale began to design and make furniture for his patrons, whom he desired to see among the most fashionable. While the ladies were so gay, the gentlemen were quite as elegant, with three-cornered hats, wigs and patches, embroidered waistcoats, with stiffened skirts to their coats, knee-breeches, silk stockings, and snuff-boxes. Such modish people could not bestow themselves comfortably in chairs with arms, so chairs without arms, and tabourets, as they were called, were quite necessary for comfort. The fashionable ailment of the day, for men at least was gout, and we find designs for "gouty stools," in which the top could be raised or lowered as best suited the needs of the patient. His designs for sofas made these articles of great size; they ran from six feet nine inches to ten feet long. His ideas as to decoration seem amusing, for he mentions that the carvings on the sofa should be emblematic of Watchfulness, Assiduity, and Rest.

Wine-coolers for which Chippendale made many designs, sometimes had brass bands around them which had the effect of making them look very heavy and clumsy. Coolers of this style were round or oval, but some of better design were oblong or square. Numbers of beautiful little tea-tables, or tea-poys, as they were often called, were also made by Chippendale, and what he called in his book of designs "candle stands" were no doubt sometimes put to this use, though their height—he says they should run from three feet six inches to four feet six inches, rendered the taller ones awkward. The following image shows a very beautiful example of one of these stands richly carved. The post is three feet seven and a half inches high, and the hexagonal top has a standing rim of very delicate carving. The little tea-stand next to it has also a slight rim, and some carving on the pedestal and feet. The music-stand is not a usual piece, and has a cupboard and drawer to contain the sheets. All three pieces are of mahogany and belong to the collection at Memorial Hall, Philadelphia.

Many of these tables or stands made their way to America, for tea-drinking was a great resource for the ladies. As early as 1720 Bohea tea was selling at Philadelphia for thirty shillings a pound. Its great cost prohibited its common use, and it was not until much later that it became common, so the greatest treat that could be offered to a neighbour was a drink of tea, particularly if the proud housewife could serve it out of a tiny porcelain cup without a handle, such cups being almost as great a rarity as the tea.

The little rim which set up above the edge of the table was intended to prevent the tea furniture from falling off. These tables are occasionally seen in America in their simpler forms. There are special ones made to order for customers by Chippendale, which are seldom allowed to leave the families for which they were originally made. There are two such tea-tables made in "Chinese taste" with fretwork legs, sides to the table, and the little standing rim to protect the china. One of these tables was made for the great-grandmother of the present owner, by Chippendale, and has come down in a state of perfect preservation. It is held in England, is thirty-nine and three-eighths inches high, the top is thirty-two by twenty-one and five-eighths inches.

Chippendale, in his book, gives very elaborate directions for preparing the wood from which this fretwork carving was to be made. In order to have it as strong as possible he advises the use of three thin sheets of wood glued together, the grain to run in opposite directions, and the fret carving to be made in this. He particularly recommends this use of glued wood for such pieces as China-Cases, which were largely fretwork with pagodas on top and hanging ornaments at the sides.

Card-tables were also made in great varieties and numbers by this same maker, and his graceful designs were copied by other and less well-known makers, so that these tables, at least in "Chippendale style," are not uncommon. His card-tables were of two styles, with leaves which folded together on top when not in use, and a plain oblong table without leaves. As

Chippendale Candle, Tea and Music Stands

card-playing was one of the most fashionable pursuits of the day in England, which fashion was followed with becoming promptitude by us. It is seen that many of these tables were needed to accommodate the gay world. Those most esteemed were the kind with leaves, which could seat a larger party than the oblong ones, and which, when not in use, could be folded together and set against the wall. Both styles, when made by Chippendale, were decorated only with carving. During the last half of the eighteenth century there were probably few families who did not own at least one card-table.

Gambling at cards had always been an amusement at courts, and there were many games in vogue. Ombre had been introduced in the previous century by Catherine of Braganza, and quadrille was another favorite game of hers. Pepys under date of February 17, 1666-7, alludes to the fact that Catherine played not only on week days but on Sundays as well.

"This evening, going to the Queene's side to see the ladies, I did find the Queene, the Duchesse of York, and another or two at cards, with the room full of great ladies and men, which I was amazed at to see of a Sunday, having not believed it, but contrarily, flatly denied the same a little while since to my cosen Roger Pepys."

The next reign, that of James II., saw basset introduced, and it retained its popularity through several reigns and was still the mode when Queen Anne occupied the throne. It broke "into her hours by day as well as by night," and the drain on the privy purse was excessive, for the queen was a good loser. The Cocoa-Tree Club, at No. 64 St. James Street, London, was, during Queen Anne's reign, a regular gambling-den. Walpole says:

"Within this week there has been a cast at hazard at the Cocoa-Tree, the difference of which amounted to £180,000."

By George II.'s reign cards were universal. The preface to the "Court Gamster" says:

"Gaming has become so much the fashion that he who in company should be ignorant of the games in vogue would be reckoned low-bred and hardly fit for conversation."

The Princess Amelia Sophia, daughter of George II., was an inveterate snuff-taker as well as gambler. Horace Walpole, who was often invited to make one at her card parties, has left many graphic pictures of her. At Bath the card-tables were one of the chief attractions, and the sums of money staked during a single night seem prodigious. But of all the Georges, George IV. had the most reckless propensities. Before he was twenty-one years old he had lost £800,000, one of his boon companions being that confirmed gamester, Charles James Fox.

Almack's was a famous gambling-club, opened in 1764. The gamesters began by pulling off their velvet and embroidered coats, putting on frieze garments, and pulling leather sleeves over their lace ruffles. High-crowned, broad-brimmed straw hats were worn to shade their eyes from the light, to keep their hair from being tumbled, and perhaps to conceal their emotions.

Chippendale Card-Table

George II was still on the throne when Chippendale published his "Director," and in such a gambling age it is no wonder that he made many card-tables in order to please his patrons. Not alone at court were they in demand, but one has only to read such transcripts of the times as Jane Austen's or Miss Burney's novels to find that nearly every country family sat down of an evening to a quiet hand at cards. Following at a distance, but as well as they were able, the fashions set at court, Americans too played cards, and Chippendale's tables were sent across the ocean and were copied by colonial cabinet-makers, who by this time had become very successful workers themselves.

Contemporary letters, which describe the propensity of the ladies to play loo all day as well as all night were, no doubt, too extravagant. On the great plantations at the South, gambling was said to be a favorite diversion, and piquet, écarté, faro, hazard, and basset were played, as well as less exciting games. Besides the tables with plain polished surfaces, some were covered with a green cloth. Others had pockets to hold the counters, which were old silver Spanish pieces or were made of mother-of-pearl. These tables were valued highly, the early ones being walnut, the later mahogany. In some of the inventories already quoted mention is made of various styles of playing-cards which were imported by the gross, as well as "pearl fish," which were the fashionable counters.

On the previous page a very beautiful Chippendale card-table is shown. It is of mahogany, richly carved on the knees, and with a heavy carved moulding. It is unusual in having five legs, one of which moves out to support the second half of the top. The feet are ball-and-claw, and within the lid is lined with cloth, has depressions for counters, and also four flat panels, one at each corner, where the candlesticks stood. It belongs to Miss Sarah Frost, Rochester, N. Y., and has been in her family over 100 years.

Most of Chippendale's furniture presents certain characteristics that are easily mastered. First may be mentioned the ball-and-claw foot, and the cabriole leg which he adopted from the Dutch, and which he used so freely before he introduced the straight leg. Then the backs of his chairs are quite distinctive, whether the splats run up and down, or become cross-braces, or are elaborated into very ornamental ribbon-work. The top bar is generally extended on each end into what, for a better name, we will call "ears."

Chippendale never used inlay on any of his pieces, preferring to produce the decoration by carving. In his

Chippendale Marble-topped Table

very ornate carvings we have mentioned the long-billed bird, the falling-water effect, and the familiar ribbon-work which is often introduced into backs with such good effect. There are a number of patterns for carving shown in the designs in his book, and used by him over and over again, with which we have become well acquainted. Little carved bands were quite universally employed to decorate the rims of his card-tables, and in his fine chairs the front bar of the seat often had a shell or other ornament carved upon it. The very finest chairs by this maker are seldom found in America, though furniture was imported freely. In Smith's "History of New York" for the year 1756, two years after Chippendale published his work, there is the following statement:

"In the City of New York, through our intercourse with Europeans, we follow the London fashions, though by the time we adopt them they become disused in England. Our affluence during the late French war introduced a degree of luxury in tables, dress, and furniture with which we were before unacquainted. But still we are not so gay a people as our neighbours at Boston, and several Southern colonies."

This is the first time possibly that the descendants of the Pilgrims have gone on record as a "gay people."

When the seats of Chippendale's pieces are stuffed, it will be noticed that the material is usually drawn over the rails, and sometimes adorned with gilt-headed nails set in a pattern or straight. He says in his catalogue that he considers this the handsomer fashion; but in some cases, where the seats were covered with set work or crewel work, they were set in the wooden frame. There are two such chairs made by Chippendale and given by the fourth Duke of Marlborough in 1790 to an ancestor of the present owner. The seats of these ribbon-backed chairs were worked by the famous Sarah, Duchess of Marlborough, and are still in a fresh and blooming state of preservation. These arm-chairs are very handsomely carved, and rest on large ball-and-claw feet. The carving is not confined to the knee alone, but runs down the leg to the end of the claw. These are owned in England.

That quantities of this furniture are changing hands all the time is evident from reading the records of sales which go on at all the large auction rooms in Europe. It is safe to say that fully half of it comes to America, and that it is possible to buy here choice specimens of the works of all the famous cabinet-makers. Even the well-known Battle Abbey has been despoiled, and while much of the furniture was Flemish and German, and not of particularly good quality, there were also some pieces of both Chippendale and Adam Bros., the latter being represented by several mirrors. Chippendale chairs of undoubted authenticity bring easily at these sales $200 each, while one of distinctly inferior quality sold for $335, owing to the authenticity of its history.

At a sale of furniture held within the year at Christie's, in London, a genuine surprise was furnished when a set of mahogany Chippendale chairs brought $5,225. A few weeks later two chairs, apparently out of the same set, appeared at another sale, also at Christie's and about an hour before the sale they were withdrawn. These chairs, says the catalogue, were given by a lady to the vicar and church wardens of a parish church in Lincolnshire. The lady died, and her executors held that they were lent, not given, and the sale was stopped until the rightful ownership should be established by law. But there was also in the catalogue still another chair which was said to belong to the same set, yet which was of a different wood and more boldly carved. This chair brought but a little more than $100.

The removal of the two previously mentioned chairs from the sale, and the whole mystery which surrounds them, has given rise to wild rumours, and all kinds of reports are circulated which makes one very cautious about buying at auctions. In fact catalogues at auctions are little to be relied on, as one will often find pieces heavy with inlay, or of undoubted American make, boldly marked Chippendale, while Sheraton is made to shoulder the baldest imitations of his style and design. It must always be a matter of regret that furniture-makers so rarely signed their work. If they had realized that individual specimens would bring as much as fine paintings, they would not have left their work clouded with an uncertain pedigree.

Chippendale did not make sideboards. He made side or

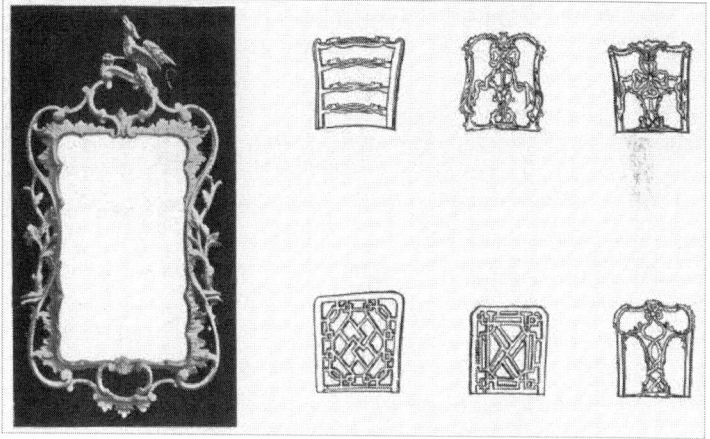

Chippendale Chair backs and Mirror-frame

serving-tables but the sideboard was a later growth, due largely to three cabinet-makers who succeeded Chippendale,—Shearer, Hepplewhite, and Sheraton, all of whom, like Chippendale, published catalogues of their designs. The nearest approach which Chippendale made to a sideboard was a table with a shallow drawer for linen. He did not make any of those pieces of furniture with drawers and cupboards which are so often called by his name.

It may be seen that on Chippendale's title-page he refers to "frames for marble slabs." These were generally tables,—side or serving tables we should call them,—and they were elaborately carved on legs and edges. Nor were they unknown in this country, for inventories as early as the middle of the eighteenth century refer to sideboard tables with marble tops, as well as marble-topped parlor tables.

Also pictured is an unusually elegant marble-topped parlor table. The profuse carving is in Chippendale's very best style, not flamboyant, but elegant and graceful. On each of the long sides is a grotesque mask, and the legs, carved over the knees with shells and flowers in low relief, end in a ball-and-paw, the hair on the foot being most delicately carved. The wood is dark, rich mahogany; the

51

marble top is of brown tint with light veinings. This fine piece is at Memorial Hall, Philadelphia.

To sum up, then, briefly, Chippendale's peculiarities may be expressed as follows:

He used the ball-and-claw foot with the cabriole leg: this was succeeded by the straight leg.

The tops of his chairs are almost invariably prolonged into little ear-like ornaments.

He never used inlay on his furniture.

He used carving as ornament, generally worked in solid mahogany for his larger pieces, and in a close-set pine which was gilded for his smaller and ornamental pieces.

Many of the gold-frame looking-glasses have the glass pane divided by delicate ornament or pilasters. This was to save expense, as in this way several small panes of glass could be used instead of one large and more costly one. The glass made in England was in very thin plates, and the bevel was ground by hand, so that it followed every twist and turn in the convolutions of the frame which rested on it.

Strength, beauty, and adaptability to the use for which the piece was made, were the watchwords for Chippendale's most characteristic furniture. It is true that during the early years of his work there was a large demand for everything French, to which he catered, yet he in time reversed this and caused the attention of the world to be drawn to England as the centre from which could be obtained the best designs in furniture. While Chippendale sought for his effects largely in his use of carving and gilding, although we find little of this latter work in the pieces seen in America, he also took the greatest pains to select brilliant and elegant brocades, wrought stuffs, and hand-worked material for the upholstered parts of his furniture. Nor did he neglect brass nails as a means of brightening up a piece, though both Hepplewhite and Sheraton used them more than he did. None of the furniture which we so fondly ascribed to his name is from the designs figured in his book, his use of brilliant metal mounts is practically unknown among us. He himself admired the beautiful Louis XIV ribbon ornament which he lavished on so many chair backs, and he says "If I may speak without vanity, they are the best I have ever seen, or perhaps have ever been made."

Like his fellow-craftsmen, Chippendale made cases for tall clocks, and some of them are odd and not in the least graceful or beautiful. One will have for ornament on the extreme top a crowing cock, life size, and rampant, the base on which he stands being a mass of ugly carving. Another has what might be called a sunburst, with a star in its midst; others have allegorical figures. His designs for mantel clocks were much prettier and in better taste everyway. He used walnut as well as mahogany for the cases, and sometimes Chinese panels, or panels painted with nymphs and goddesses, called in "French taste," were inserted. These decorations served, besides, to ornament the fire-screens which were popular pieces of

52

furniture. He made designs for chimney-pieces or "over-mantels." These were filled in with glass. Chippendale says:

"Chimney-pieces require great care in the execution. The embossments must be very bold, the foliage neatly laid down, and the whole properly relieved. The top may be gilt, as likewise some other ornamental parts."

Knowing the sturdy, plain characteristics of Chippendale's furniture as we see it, this constant reference to gilt and the mass of over-decoration seems quite out of place. His beds were called Canopy beds, Chinese beds, Dome beds, Gothic beds with flat testers, Field beds, Tent beds, Sofa beds with canopies, and the usual high four-posters.

Many beautiful clothes-presses were made by Chippendale, either chest like affairs on four legs, or having drawers below and wardrobe above, some of these latter bearing a strong resemblance to the French pieces from which they were copied.

Scant mention is made of Chippendale, in contemporary literature, but he has the distinction accorded to but few of having a large class of furniture design called by his name, instead of being designated by the period in which it was made. Mr. Clouston, in his book on "Chippendale Furniture" says that there were two Chippendales, father and son, and alludes to the author of the "Director" as "the elder Mr. Chippendale". The son, like many sons of great men, seems to have lost his identity in the reputation which has been gradually gathering about his father's name. He seems to have produced nothing of moment, and the family has sunk again into the obscurity from which one man had the genius to raise it.

Adam, Sheraton, Hepplewhite and Empire Era Furnishings

THE increased market offered to English merchants in the colonies, now more prosperous, produced in quick succession several cabinet-makers who worked in a different style from Chippendale, and made much very handsome furniture. Robert and James Adam, by training and profession architects, turned their attention to furniture which would be appropriate in rooms of Greek or Roman style. Their designs were all on classic lines, and were beautifully painted besides by the popular artists of the day, like Angelica Kauffmann and Pergolese, who, like Alma Tadema in our day, did not hesitate to expend their art upon fine pieces of furniture.

The Adam brothers introduced the use of composition ornaments coloured and gilded, which were really a revival of the Italian process of "gesso," and which they had learned during their years of study in Italy. They designed many mantelpieces, also decorated in classic style, and had a decided influence in moulding the taste of their contemporaries and successors. Satin-wood was introduced by them, or at least at this period, and was

A reproduced piece in the Adams style, during the late 19th century revival period - Image: Clem Rutter

used for inlaying as well as for the manufacture of whole pieces of furniture. Most of it, when used as the wood of the entire piece, is decorated with medallions of marquetry of some darker wood, as tulip, rosewood, or mahogany.

The Adam brothers did not make any furniture themselves, but had it made by popular makers under their personal direction. Later in this part are shown three chairs of Adam design. The side chair retains its original covering of a heavy wool plush, with classic figures stamped in it of wreaths and maces. Its covering was also designed by Adam. This chair and the arm-chair like it are very delicately carved in low relief with a small leaf pattern. The legs are fluted and end in a form of spade-foot. The arm-chair on the top is very richly carved, and the entire woodwork is gilded. The covering has been restored. These three chairs are in the Museum connected with Cooper Institute.

In 1764 Robert Adam published his book dedicated to George III., and illustrated with most elaborate engravings by Bartolozzi and other fashionable engravers. For this graceful act Robert Adam was appointed architect to the king, and his rise was rapid and brilliant. James Adam had now completed his studies and was taken into partnership by his brother. In 1773 they began to publish engravings of their architectural works in serial parts. They continued to issue these until 1778, when the entire work was

Room in Whipple House, Ipswich, Mass.

published under the title of "Works in Architecture by Robert and James Adam Esquires." It contains quite as many designs for furniture as some of the so-called furniture catalogues.

While the outlines of the furniture are very graceful and delicate, their beauty is much increased by the skilful and artistic paintings of Angelica Kauffmann and Zucchi by which they are embellished. Pergolese was brought from Italy to add still further to the beauty of their work. John Flaxman, at this time creating lovely classic designs in various kinds of wares for Wedgwood, also contributed to their success, and many of his plaques and panels were set in their furniture to its further adornment. They were used not only in satin-wood, but in other furniture as well which was painted in the same colours as the Wedgwood ware. Whole rooms, walls, ceiling, and furniture were coloured to match, even the harpsichord and candle-stands being painted and decorated with Wedgwood plaques. Of the second book,

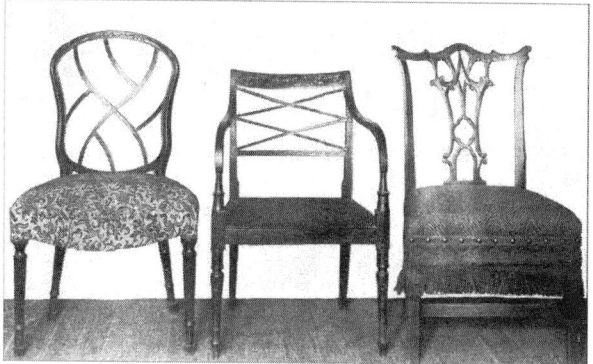

Chippendale, Sheraton and Hepplewhite Chairs

furniture designs fill one volume, mirrors another, and girandoles a third.

55

Robert Adam showed wonderful skill and aptitude in adapting classic forms to modern taste, and his pieces are never overloaded with ornament, but retain simple, graceful lines. He never considered any detail too small for his minute attention. Besides designing the woodwork of his furniture he also drew the patterns for the stuffs to cover them; even the little silk cushions on the arms of the chairs had the same care bestowed on them as the backs and seat. When he designed a bed, the counterpane to go on it was also made under his direction or designed by him. A little bag to hang on a lady's arm was not too slight an object to be made beautiful by his artistic hand. He paid the greatest attention to having the covering for upholstered furniture appropriate to the style of chair it went on, but he allowed himself great latitude in gilding, and, as we have already said, in painting his furniture in colours. He also gave variety to his tables by the use of coloured marble tops. The Adam brothers designed some of the interior fittings for "Strawberry Hill." They also built Colzean Castle, designed Alnwick Castle, and many other splendid homes.

Thomas Shearer is a name not often heard in America, yet the book, "The London Cabinet-Maker's Book of Prices," published in 1788, contained many beautiful designs by him. This work provided more for the cabinet-maker himself than for the gentleman, to whom most of the previous works of this nature had been dedicated. There were many members of the London Cabinet-Maker's Society, but only three made the illustrations to the book,—Thomas Shearer, Hepplewhite, and a man named Casement, who furnished but two. Now, when there are so many banks and safe-deposit companies, we do not feel the need of secret

Adam Chairs

drawers and repositories for storing our valuables. They were quite necessary a hundred years or more ago and much ingenuity was expended in concealing them from curious or prying eyes. We are also wont to consider recent times and conditions responsible for such shams and mockeries as folding beds, and articles of furniture that are not what they seem. In these early books of designs are not only folding beds, press-beds, and library bedsteads, but folding washstands and toilet-tables, as well as tables, toilets, and bureaus which concealed the mattress and bed furniture by day.

56

Some of these pieces were most elaborate and had intricate machinery to work them. A graceful, classical urn of wood, touched on the right spot, would open and disclose a basin and ewer, while a writing-table could be unfolded into a lady's dressing-table with folding glasses, and boxes for the necessary powder, pomatum, brushes and pins.

To Thomas Shearer we are indebted for that useful article, the sideboard, which has assumed such a variety of forms, and among his designs were dressing, card, and tea-tables, of many styles, and various desks, but he designed no chairs. Many of his pieces bear a close resemblance to those of Sheraton. Between the severity of the latest period of

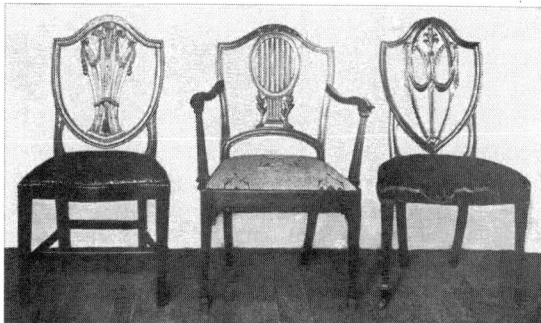

Hepplewhite Chairs

Chippendale and the dainty designs of Sheraton, Shearer and Hepplewhite find their place, though neither of them ever approached in beauty of design, or in popularity, Chippendale who preceded them or Sheraton who succeeded them.

A. Hepplewhite's book, "The Cabinet-Maker and Upholsterer's Guide, or Repository of Designs for Every Article of Household Furniture in the Newest and Most Approved Taste," was published in 1789 and contained three hundred designs for pieces of furniture which have been so often copied that they have grown familiar to us. His chairs are extremely pretty, but, unlike those of Chippendale, who sought solidity and careful construction, Hepplewhite's chairs were so faulty and fragile in construction that they broke easily. Up to this time the splat had joined the back of the chair and served to make it much stronger, but Hepplewhite never brought it down to the seat, usually having it curved and joining the side rails three or four inches above the seat.

There are more pieces of Hepplewhite furniture in America than one is aware of. His chairs are by no means uncommon, and are very easily recognized by their peculiar backs. His tables, with the delicate inlay and slender tapering legs, as also his sideboards, are frequently called by the name of his great successor, Sheraton, and even in England the two makers are frequently confused. He had a specialty of his own,—that of japanned or lacquered furniture, and the patterns he most frequently employed were fruit and flowers on a black ground. Paintings such as these were taught to young ladies as an accomplishment at school, and no doubt many of them tried their "prentice" hands on some nice old mahogany piece as soon as they got home.

Hepplewhite had another peculiarity in his preference for using a circle or some portion of it in his designs. On looking over his "Guide" one will notice that a half circle was often used as the design for a sideboard, or table to be set against the wall. His small tables are nearly always round or a broad oval, and his chair-backs follow the same shape, so did his girandoles and tea-trays. For a central ornament to his chair backs he frequently carved three Prince's feathers, or drooping ears of wheat, neither of which design is particularly pleasing. Besides the circular he used also the shield-shaped back. On the previous page is shown three of his characteristic chairs. The one on the left has the Prince's feathers, and all of them show the slender leg which in two of them ends in the spade-foot.

The dining-tables of this period, before the days of the extension table, had round, square, or octagonal tops, supported on a column which rested on a plinth having several carved feet. There were a number of variations of the arrangement of feet. In order to accommodate a large party several of these tables could be placed together, and when not in use could be placed against the wall to serve as side-tables. His easy chairs—and he made many of these, large and comfortable—he covered entirely with upholstery, no woodwork showing but the legs.

In the Hepplewhite and Shearer pieces the noticeable feature of decoration is the inlay, often of two or three coloured woods and in a variety of designs. Many kinds of wood were employed at this time in inlay or marquetry work, besides all the familiar ones Shearer mentions,—"tulip, rose, snake, panella," etc., and later lilac-wood also was used. The husk pattern was very popular at this period for an inlay pattern, and Wedgwood also used it

Hepplewhite Card Table

frequently in his splendid jasper pottery. It resembles the husks of oats when ripe, the spreading of the two halves allowing the pattern to be used over and over again.

In Shearer's work, as well as Hepplewhite's, a slender tapering leg is much in use, inlaid down about half its length, often with satin-wood or holly, and sometimes with ebony as well. Many of the sideboards made in America were on English models, and they are veneered on pine, the back and drawers being made of this same wood. There are many variations of shape,—what are known as serpentine and swell fronts being quite usual, the handles being the oval ones which are so common on all varieties of pieces with drawers, and there is also a fan-shaped piece of inlay which will frequently be seen. The position of this is not always the same, it may be found in the corners of closets, and long bottle-drawers, or it may be inserted as a sort of brace between the bottom of the sideboard and the legs. Hepplewhite was very fond of inlaying a band of holly or satin-wood around the legs of his pieces, three or four inches from the ground. It will be found on his sideboards, card-tables and desks, and is generally about an inch wide. His book was one of the most valuable ever given to English cabinet-makers. His individuality of shape is always pleasing, even if he did not concern himself about making his furniture structurally correct. He claims, and indeed with absolute correctness, "to unite elegance with utility and blend the useful with the agreeable."

On the previous page is shown one of a pair of card-tables, Hepplewhite design, made of mahogany and inlaid with ebony and satin-wood. They belong to Mr. William M. Hoyt of Rochester, N. Y.

Like Adam, Hepplewhite made great use of satin-wood for whole pieces of furniture. He used his well-known and characteristic shapes in chair-backs and little sofas, cabinets and workstands, table stands, harpsichord cases, and commodes. Satin-wood had been but recently introduced from the East Indies and was instantly popular. Even mantelpieces were made of it, to match the furniture, and there was a fancy to have the drawing-rooms and boudoirs very light and elegant. Clothes had shrunk in dimensions, no more hoops and farthingales embarrassed their wearers, the stiffness was banished from coat-tails, and consequently the furniture had shrunk too. Chairs were small and narrow, and window-seats, made in abundance by Hepplewhite, were deservedly popular, and the coverings were in accord with the gaiety of the woodwork. Figure 32 shows two Hepplewhite settees with shield-shaped backs. The upper one is of mahogany with low relief carvings on the tops, and the lower of satin-wood, with cane seat and the woodwork beautifully painted. The elegance of

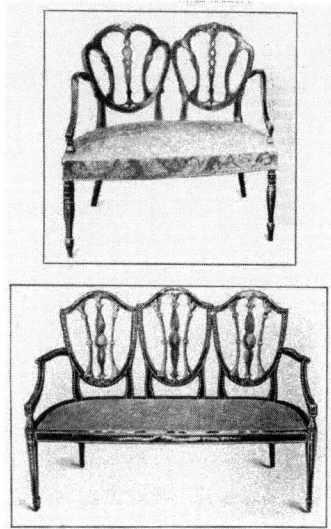

Hepplewhite Settees

this painted satin-wood has long been admired. Unfortunately it has caught the popular taste, and it is now reproduced in such large quantities that it is freely offered for sale by dealers in our large cities. The pieces shown in our illustration are both fine specimens of the original maker and are owned by the Waring Galleries, London.

It was no longer necessary to make the legs of chairs of such stout proportions, and as the bodies of the chairs were lighter so the legs dwindled exceedingly and were given only a semblance of solidity by the use of the "spade-foot" so much affected by Hepplewhite. Their appearance of fragility was farther enhanced by groovings and flutings, but they are always pretty.

Although his characteristic chairs have shield-shaped or oval backs, he gives in his book eighteen designs of bannister-backed chairs, to be carried out in

59

mahogany. The general dimensions given by Hepplewhite for his chairs are as follows:

"Width in front, 20 inches; depth of seat, 17 inches; height of seat frame, 17 inches; total height, about 37 inches."

He gives most definite directions about coverings. Mahogany chairs should have the seats of horsehair, plain, striped, checkered, etc., according to taste; or cane bottoms with cushions which should

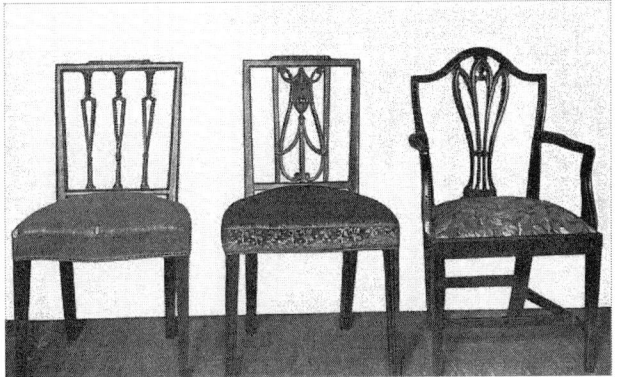

Sheraton Chairs

be covered with the same material as the bed and window curtains. He was fond of the "Duchess," which consisted of two Barjeer or arm-chairs with a stool between them, all three pieces fitting together at pleasure and making a lounge from six to eight feet long. His press-beds vary little in appearance from wardrobes, but it was in smaller and daintier pieces that his particular talent found play. His knife-boxes are extremely elegant, particularly when in urn shape with a rod in the centre to prevent the top of the urn from being removed. All the handles and knobs on his larger pieces of furniture are round, but on sideboards frequently oval, his double chests of drawers have either French or block feet.

Tripod reading-desks, urn-stands, beautiful tea-trays, caddies and tea-chests are richly inlaid or painted. We find him not only making very ornate and richly inlaid card-tables, but "Pembroke tables" as well, with either round or square tops. Such tables have leaves, but, instead of the legs moving out to support the leaves, small arms come out from the table-frame.

His writing-tables and desks have tambour tops, that is strips of wood pasted on cloth, so that they roll back into receptacles provided for them, and are filled with secret drawers and flat cupboards for deeds or papers. Among his other small pieces which are distinguished by their grace are dressing-glasses, shaving-tables with glasses and without, "bason" stands, designs for brackets, fire-screens, wash-hand-stands, cornices, lamps, girandoles, and looking-glasses. His larger designs show dressing-tables and bureaus with curved and swell fronts, beds, four-posters, and field-beds with very graceful sweeps and much variety of design. His stuffed furniture is comfortable in the extreme, and the tall easy chairs with cheek pieces must have been well calculated to protect from searching draughts. Many of these easy chairs found their way to America, and as their cost was not extortionate moderate homes enjoyed them as well as wealthy ones.

After the Revolution, in all the seaboard towns and the more settled places near cities, there was a still greater call for all styles and luxuries popular in England. Indeed the former Colonies presented very curious and marked contrasts, being, as it is tersely put, "rolling in wealth or dirt poor." In Philadelphia there had been much style and "gentility" for many years. The English officers had, no doubt, brought some comforts with them, and they found others awaiting them. Major Andrés letter describing supper at the "Mischianza," May 18, 1778, gives a vivid picture of the festivities of the times.

Sheraton Desk

—"At twelve, supper was announced, and the large folding-doors being suddenly thrown open discovered a magnificent salon of 210 feet long by 40 feet wide, and 22 in height, with three alcoves on each side which served for sideboards. Fifty-six large pier-glasses ornamented with green silk artificial flowers and ribbands; one hundred branches with three lights in each trimmed in the same manner as the mirrors; eighteen lustres each with twenty-four lights suspended from the ceiling and ornamented as the branches.

Three hundred wax tapers disposed along the supper-tables, four hundred and thirty covers, twelve hundred dishes, twenty-four black slaves in Oriental dresses with silver-collars and bracelets ranged in two lines, and bending to the ground as the General Howe and the Admiral appeared together."

All the lustres, mirrors, etc., with which the room was adorned, were borrowed, says Watson, from the townsfolk, and all were returned uninjured.

Eighty-four families kept carriages in 1772, and writing as late as 1802, Dr. Michaud calls Philadelphia—

—"At present the largest, the handsomest, and the most populous city of the United States. The streets are paved, and are provided with broad bricked footways. Pumps, placed on each side of them at about one hundred yards from each other, supply an abundance of water."

Dolly Madison, writing in 1791 of the fashions of the day in Philadelphia, says:

"Very long trains are worn, and they are festooned up with loops and bobbin and small covered buttons, the same as the dress. The hats are quite a different shape from what they used to be. The bonnets are all open on the top, through which the hair is passed, either up or down as you fancy, though latterly they wear it more up than down; it is quite out of fashion to frizz or curl the hair."

Salem, in Massachusetts, with her vessels touching at every port, was already becoming known for her luxury, her teak-wood as well as her mahogany furniture, her china and plate. Enough of these still remain to show her importance and the elegance of her homes. But there was another side to this picture. Here is the description of the home of a settler away from any of the large centres, Charles Rich, of Vermont, member of Congress, began housekeeping as late as 1791. All his household possessions were valued at $66.00. He writes:

"I constructed at the mill a number of household articles of furniture which have been in daily use from that time to the present."

The newest styles were of small importance in such surroundings as these, and luxuries passed slowly along pioneer roads; yet every ship coming to American ports brought furniture, stuffs, plate, and china to tempt the wealth of those who could afford them, and among such were pieces made by Sheraton, the fashionable cabinet-maker who came on the scene late enough to profit by the designs of his predecessors. Indeed he is most frankly pleased with his own skill and artistic taste, and in his long preface sets forth the merits of his own book and discredits all those before him. He considers his

Sideboard

book much superior because he gives drawings in perspective. Much of the book is a very dry dissertation on geometry. Its second half gives descriptions of furniture, of the various styles, and the uses of the pieces. He says in his Introduction:

"The design of this part of the Book is intended to exhibit the present taste of furniture, and at the same time give the workman some assistance in the manufacturing part of it."

Sheraton's early furniture is distinguished by great elegance of design, fine construction, and graceful ornament. The legs of his pieces are slender and straight, as distinguished from the cabriole leg, but are generally enriched with flutings, and they taper pleasingly to the foot. While he uses carving, it is generally applied in low relief and does not interfere with the lines of construction. His preference is, like Hepplewhite's, for ornamenting with inlay of woods of different colours and decorating with brass. The fine proportions of his early furniture, the simple shapes clearly defined, and its structural beauty where each part is doing its work, render it admirable in every way.

A simple desk of Sheraton pattern is shown. It is of mahogany, and the doors of the upper part open, revealing pigeon-holes and drawers. The flat top over the drawers opens out on rests, making a broad, flat desk top. The brasses and key-scutcheons are original, and the moulding of the drawers overlaps.

After 1793 Sheraton made little furniture, but gave his time chiefly to writing his furniture books. For the patterns used in his inlay he had recourse to classic models for his inspiration, like the Adam brothers, who had done much to popularize this simplicity of design. Sheraton used urns, rosettes, festoons, scrolls, and pendant

Sofa, Sheraton Style

flowers as his favorite decorations. The simple curves of which many of these are composed lent themselves admirably to inlay, and the harmony of the colours of the woods gave a grace to this form of ornament and suits it exactly to the furniture on which it finds a place.

Sheraton wrote several works on furniture and upholstery. The first one published in 1791, was "The Cabinet-Maker and Upholsterer's Drawing Book." This was followed by "Designs for Household Furniture" in 1804, and he had not completed his "Cabinet-Maker, Upholsterer, and General Artist's Encyclopedia" in 1807. He gave directions for making, among other things, folding-beds, washstands, card-tables, sideboards, and many other pieces. He frequently employed the lyre as a design for his chair-backs, as well as supports for tables. In chairs it often has strings of brass; on the tables it takes heavier and more substantial form.

Sheraton's beds seem almost as impossible as Chippendale's. He, too, made alcove, sofa, or couch beds. He also gave designs for "summer beds" made in two compartments (we should call them "twin beds,") but both are included under a frame or canopy, and the whole affair is very cumbersome and heavy. His chairs, tables, and sideboards are the pieces by which we know him best and in which he is most admirable. He says himself, in regard to drawing-room chairs, that many are finished in white and gold, or that the ornaments may be japanned, but that the French finish them in mahogany with gilt mouldings. Sheraton made very dainty designs for tripod stands, fire-screens and ladies' desks, with tambour doors. Also "bason"-stands with tambour doors and writing-desks with curved cylinder tops, which tops fell into the space behind the pigeon-holes and drawers. Wash-hand tables had also these curved cylinder tops, and all furniture which was put to toilet purposes was so arranged that it would look like something else, and transform a bedroom into a boudoir. These cylinder-topped pieces were designed as early as 1792.

In furniture, as in art, there are no absolutely abrupt changes, but one style is overshadowed by another as Chippendale gradually overcame the rococo and stood for an individual style. Hepplewhite influenced Sheraton very much, although the latter declares in one of his books, published two years later than Hepplewhite's, that the latter's designs have become quite antiquated. Such a piece of furniture is seen in the sideboard-table or sideboard shown above. It was undoubtedly made by one of

Sheraton Sideboard

these two men, and it is difficult to decide which. The form of foot is more common to Hepplewhite than to Sheraton, and the inlaid border of satin-wood is wider than he was wont to use. The brass rail at the back was used to support silver or porcelain dishes. The handles are original and the wood mahogany. This handsome piece belongs to the Waring Galleries, London.

Horsehair was used for covering by both makers, and in both cases gilt-headed nails put in a festoon were used to fasten it down. Sheraton's first style was much the most pleasing. It was distinguished by a delicacy and an elegance which were entirely lost in his later designs, which were so strongly influenced by the Empire style. The first illustration in his "Cabinet Maker's and Upholsterer's Book" is what he calls a "Universal table," to be made of mahogany, and which at will may be converted into a dining-table, or, by pulling out a drawer, discover all the compartments necessary for storing kitchen condiments, such as sugar and spices, etc.

The sofa depicted shows this merging into Empire style, for the legs are heavier than those we are accustomed to, and the carved pineapple appears on the arm instead of the more delicate carving seen on earlier chairs and sofas. The covering is hair-cloth fastened down with brass nails. This sofa stood for many years in the Old Manse at Concord, Mass. It belonged to the Rev. Ezra Ripley, who came to Concord as pastor in 1778. Times were unsettled and currency was depreciated, so that when his salary of five hundred and fifty pounds was paid it was found to be worth just forty pounds. To make up this deficiency Dr. Ripley did a man's work in the fields.

For years he laboured at tilling the ground at least three days in a week and sometimes even more. He was an ardent man, and from his moral worth was often known as "Holy Ripley." This sofa, uneasy as it looks to modern eyes, perhaps seemed luxurious to him after a day at the plough. The cover which it wears is said to be the original one, and if this is true its condition is so good that I fear the sofa was kept permanently in the "south parlor" or the "north parlor," as the best room was called in those days, and the good man was given nothing easier to rest on than a wooden Windsor chair, or a straight-backed rush-bottomed one, or perhaps the kitchen settle.

With the introduction and extended use of the sideboard came several articles to be used in connection with it, to which Sheraton turned his attention. Among these may be mentioned knife and spoon-boxes, which were of several different designs. Sheraton apparently did not

Sheraton Sideboard – No. 2

make these knife-boxes himself, but only designed them, for he says,

"As these cases are not made in regular cabinet shops it may be of service to mention where they may be executed in the best taste by one who makes it his main business, i. e. John Lane, No. 44, St. Martin's-le-Grand, London."

Two pretty ones, as well as two wine-coolers, are shown on the first image of the Sheraton sideboard. This sideboard has two little closets with tambour doors at the bottom, and deep wine-drawers on the sides. There is the brass rail similar to the Sheraton desk pictured earlier.

One of the handsomest knife-boxes is an urn-shaped one which has been noted as made also by Hepplewhite. It is wrought in mahogany, the veneer made in pie-shaped pieces, each bit being outlined with a delicate line of holly

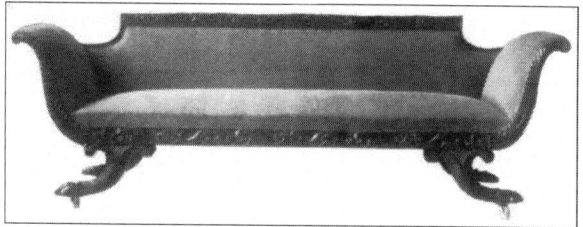

Empire Sofa

wood. The knives were held in a perforated rack inside, with the handles up, and a pair of these boxes on either end of the sideboard made a very ornamental finish.

65

Another shape also in vogue was more box-like in shape, the cover sloping toward the front. Not only knives, but spoons also, were held in the racks with which the interior was fitted; and as these latter were put in bowls up, the cases, when open, showed to excellent advantage the worldly wealth of the household, and were ornamental besides. Sometimes the covers of these boxes set back flat against a portion of the top, and made a tray on which could be placed silver cups, mugs, posset-pots, ewers, or any pieces of table silver of moderate size. Then there were the wine-boxes, or wine-coolers as they were often called, handsome massive boxes of wood, generally mahogany, or whatever wood the sideboard was made of. They stood beneath it, or, if the sideboard was low, at one side. The usual number of bottles they contained was from four to a dozen. General Washington's wine-box has room for eighteen bottles. There are still a dozen of the original bottles in it, holding a gallon each. We should call them decanters, for they are of handsome cut glass.

There is a letter from General Washington to Colonel Hamilton in the possession of Major Church of Rochester, N. Y., presenting him with a wine-cooler, "holding six bottles ... one of four which I imported during my term of governmental administration."

A more usual style of sideboard, Sheraton pattern, is that given in the image on the previous page. This handsome and useful piece of furniture had its counterparts in many of the stately old houses from the Carolinas up. It is of the swell-front type and has five deep drawers and a closet. The wood is mahogany and without inlay. This sideboard is at the Whipple House, Ipswich, Mass.

After the French Revolution of 1790 furniture became markedly different. Greek models were chosen once more; the tripod

Empire Sofa No. 2

became a favorite support. Mahogany was freely used, but so were coarse woods, in which case they were carved and profusely gilded. The most valuable book, for cabinet-makers, on "Empire" furniture, was published by the architects Percier and Fontaine in 1809. It was not filled with fanciful designs merely, as we have seen was the case with some of the catalogues of English makers, but every design shown in it had been carried out before it was published. Many of the drawings were adapted from classic models preserved in the Vatican. In many ways this style has not much to recommend it. It is apt to be heavy and stiff, particularly when made by English makers. The French decorated it with exquisite forms in metal (treated in another chapter), but the English contented themselves with cast brass. It was far preferable under the manipulation of American cabinet-makers, who restricted the use of brass and allowed the handsome woods to show themselves to the best advantage. The Dutch, who also were not behind hand in the adoption of this and Napoleonic style, made tables, secretaries, chairs, etc., severe and regular in form, but enriched with their admirable marquetry, and with heads and feet of animals sparingly used. Sheraton and Shearer were swept along by the tide of fashion and drew Empire designs.

Gillow, the inventor of the extension-table, whose firm was established as early as 1800, made many fine designs and had orders from the best patrons. His firm is still carried on under the same name.

In 1808 George Smith was made "Upholder Extraordinary to H. R. H., the Prince of Wales." He published a book, of course, having a hundred and fifty-eight designs. They included bedsteads, tables, chairs, bookcases and commodes, and other articles of furniture copied from the French, like escritoires, jardinières, chiffonièrs, showing how the fancy for French things was increasing. He gives very definite rules as to how and when to use various woods.

Pier Table

—"Mahogany, when used in houses of consequence, should be confined to the parlour and bed-chamber floors.

"In furniture for these apartments the less inlay of other woods, the more chaste will be the style of work. If the wood be of a fine compact and bright quality, the ornaments may be carved clean in the mahogany. Where it may be requisite to make out panelling by inlay of lines, let these be of brass or ebony.

"In drawing-rooms, boudoirs, ante-rooms, East and West India satin-wood, rosewood, tulip-wood, and the other varieties of woods brought from the East, may be used. With satin and light-coloured woods the decorations may be of ebony or rosewood; with rosewood let the decorations be ormolu and the inlay of brass."

The first and very handsome sofa of carved mahogany, Empire style, is pictured before it had arrived at its heaviest stage. The carving is extremely handsome, both rails of seat and back being decorated with dolphins. The foot is of the bear shape, and the arms are graceful in curve. This piece is of English make.

While we miss in the late Empire styles—say from 1810 to 1825—much of the lightness and grace which had been contributed by the carving and inlay which were so freely used in the preceding period, yet there was a solidity and massive dignity which was not without a certain charm. Then, too, these pieces were generally veneered, and in them the beautiful grain of the mahogany, which was the favorite wood, showed to greatest advantage. The sofa second sofa on the previous page is such a piece. It is of unusual length, the top of the arm is stuffed, thus doing away with "squabs," as the cushions which were used on sofas, long and narrow, were called.

The wood, which is largely shown, is of that dark rich hue inclined to red, with veining many shades darker, and it is in a fine state of preservation. This piece belongs to Anthony Killgore, Esq., Flemington, N. J.

To about the same period does the pier-table on the previous page belong which is not usual in design, because of the third pier which starts from a circular shelf in the middle of the base. The swan piers at each end are very graceful, and the handsome grain of the mahogany is shown to great advantage.

Empire Sideboard

This piece belongs to the Misses Killgore, of Flemington, N. J., as does the sideboard shown above. The doors of the lower part, with the fan, are solid mahogany, the carving on the legs and ornamental scrolls is fine. The middle of the top is raised to permit the insertion of a looking-glass, and the capitals at the tops of the pillars are of fine brass-work. Above the middle drawer, a shelf draws out for use in serving meals. The whole sideboard sets back on a little shelf above the bear's feet, a feature not unusual in the finer boards of this period.

Empire style bookcase - circa 1830-1840 - Image: Cincinnati Art Museum

The surroundings of this fine old piece of furniture are in keeping with its importance, the china showing above it on the wall being the Staffordshire blue made during the first quarter of the nineteenth century, while the mirror directly above it is of equal age.

Environment has a great deal to do with bringing out the true beauties of this stately old furniture. It must be surrounded with objects of approximate age and of equal dignity, otherwise it looks as unseemly as an ancient dame with a pink rose in her hair. The work-table shown belongs to the same period, but of a little earlier date than the last pieces shown. The legs are richly carved, as is the central pillar. This also belongs to the Misses Killgore.

Not many pieces of such solidity were required in a room, and in those days overloading did not stand for elegance. In 1800, when the spacious Tayloe house in Washington was built, the furniture of the great drawing-room was a set of ash, sixteen pieces. There were twelve chairs with chintz cushions, and two card-tables; there were also a centre table and one upholstered couch, and a settee, but not one so-called easy-chair. Much furniture like that shown in Figures 40-43, is to be found in the old houses of such places as Cherry Valley, N. Y., where there is little changing about, and furniture has descended from one generation to another and still stands in its old familiar home.

Empire Work-Table

Colonial and Later Periods

UNDER the broad head of Colonial Furniture may really be classed all the "movables and chattels" which belonged to the early settlers, while to be entirely correct, this characterization belongs only to such furniture as was brought in or made before 1776. As the pioneers came from many lands, so many different kinds of furniture will be included in the list.

We must begin at the South, with the melancholy little plantation at Jamestown. Through evil times the feeble colony struggled, harassed by poverty, disease, savage foes, and internal dissensions. There in 1607 were planted the first beginnings of the settlements which were in three hundred years to cover a continent. Traces of the little colony have almost disappeared now by the action of the James River, high tide covering the brick foundations of the ancient buildings. Walking along the shore one may find little red and white clay pipes, in smoking which, filled with the fragrant weed, the pioneers forgot their woes. Glass beads striped like gooseberries, to take the eyes of the Indians in barter, pieces of water-soaked brick from these toil-built houses, and even traces of the days of Smith, sword-hilts, bits of armour, balls, etc., and—more pathetic mementos of Jamestown's trials—human bones and coffin-handles.

Yet in 1639, thirty-two years after the foundation of the colony, there were in Maryland some planters called "rich," who measured their worldly goods by their value in tobacco, the raising of which weed had proved their only salvation. The laws regarding its cultivation, particularly in Massachusetts, were very stringent. It was only to be grown as medicine and used privately. It was considered a more harmful indulgence than liquor, and the "Creature called Tobacko" was hemmed and hedged about with rules and

Kitchen at Deerfield, Mass.

restrictions. It circumvented them all, was planted and grown, and finally became a commodity of much value and a medium of exchange. About ninety years later we find an item which shows how universal had become its use. The will of May Bickley, attorney general of the province of New York, filed April 27, 1724, directs that he "wishes to be buried without pipes and tobacco as is usual."

To Maryland and Virginia were transplanted almost bodily rich homes from the mother country, filled with the luxuries to which their occupants had been accustomed. It has been said that many of the grand old homes in the South were built of "English brick." While this is true in the letter, it is entirely misleading to the reader in general. The bricks were not brought from England, because at that time there were few ships afloat capable of bearing any such quantity as would have been necessary for a house of any considerable size. Mr. McCrady, in his "History of South Carolina," has taken considerable pains to explain how this error arose. The historic Miles Brewton house, now called the Pringle house built about 1770 in the city of Charleston, is one of the best known houses in the State. It was used as military headquarters during both the Revolutionary and the Civil wars. It has been computed, by actual measurement, that the house contains 1,278,720 bricks. Each of these weighs eight pounds, the whole amounting to 4,566 tons. No vessels then afloat could carry more than 500 tons, so it would have taken nine of such vessels to bring over the bricks for this house alone. Josiah Quincy says in his Journal that this house cost about $50,000, which sum would hardly have covered the expense of so many vessels from London. Mr. McCrady's solution is that there were two styles of brick made, one, large and heavy, known as "English" the other called "Dutch" which were very small.

There were, however, bricks brought from England, for the prices of brick, both of British and New England make, were fixed by statute. As early as 1662 brickmakers and bricklayers were paid by each thousand bricks made and laid by them. The first material brought into Virginia for building purposes was in 1607, for the use of George Percy. Brickmakers were twice advertised for in 1610, and joiners were at work on the furniture needed for the new homes.

The houses late in the seventeenth century were by no means so large as one would expect. Six or eight rooms was the usual size, and many had even fewer. The house of Cornelius Lloyd, whose estate was valued at 131,044 pounds of tobacco, contained a chamber and hall and a kitchen with loft and dairy. The windows were often but sliding panels, but in houses of any pretensions glass was used. In 1684 Colonel Byrd sent to London for 400 feet of glass, with drawn lead and solder in proportion. Robert Beverly, Sr., one of the richest men in the Virginia colony prior to the opening of the eighteenth century, had in his dining-hall one oval and one folding table, a leather couch, two chests, a chest of drawers and fifteen Russia-leather chairs, value £9 9s. His supply of table linen was abundant, and the table-ware was pewter, with wooden trenchers and some earthenware. Richard Hobbs, of Rappahannock, who died in 1667, owned, among much household stuff, but a single fork, John Frison, of Henrico County had one of tortoise-shell. Robert Dudley, of Middlesex County who died in 1700, had several forks made of horn.

To show some of the luxuries for sale in Virginia prior to 1670 the inventory of the store of John Frison, mentioned above, is given.

"Holland night-caps; muslin neck-cloths; silk-fringed gloves; silver shoe-buckles; embroidered Holland waistcoats; 2 doz. pr. white gloves; 1 lace cap; 7 lace shirts; 9 lace ruffles; holster-caps of scarlet embroidered with silver and gold; gold and silver hat-bands; a parcel of silver lace; and a feathered velvet cap."

There were also many valuable furs.

Mrs. Diggs, widow of the governor of Virginia, died in 1699. She was a person of much consequence in the colony, and her inventory is interesting on that account. In her hall parlour were—

—"5 Spanish tables; 2 green and two Turkey-worked carpets; 9 Turkey-worked chairs, and 11 with arrows woven on the seats; 1 embroidered and 1 Turkey-worked couch; 5 pictures (valued at five shillings); 2 pairs of brass andirons; 3 pr. old tongs; and 1 clock."

William Penn's Table

Not only did English ships bring on every voyage the best that England afforded, but Dutch traders, too, crowded in with their own goods, and others besides from the East. The inventories mention "Dutch cases", and "Dutch turned chairs", before 1680; and as these rich planters had tobacco to trade, they obtained all the luxuries to be had. It is seen that New England had her rich and prosperous men also, and some fine homes were built as early as 1639. Earlier in the book, we showed a room in the famous old Whipple House, Ipswich, Mass., built about 1642.

The solidity of these houses is exemplified by the beams, with their finely moulded edges. The furniture is both interesting and beautiful, one of the most attractive pieces being the desk made on Sheraton lines which stands on the right-hand side. A handsome bookcase and desk fill the corner, and a little Pembroke table holds much glass.

The picture shows a typical New England kitchen in Colonial times. It has been arranged in the Deerfield Memorial Hall, and all the furniture and utensils shown herein were gathered in the neighbourhood. These primitive homes did not have mantelpieces as a rule, but the heavy wooden beam fashioned with an axe was called the mantel-tree.

The one shown here did duty for a hundred and sixty-eight years. The wide chimney-piece could easily accomodate the small children of the family sitting on billets of wood, while the elders were comfortable on the settle with its high backboard. It has a convenient candle-bracket which could be adjusted to suit the reader, and if more light were needed the candle-stand was convenient. The back of this settle is sixty inches high, more than is usual. It was owned by Jacob Rich, who settled in the neighbourhood of Deerfield, Mass., in 1777.

A famous house was known as the "Old Stone House" at Guilford, Conn., while at Boston, Salem, Danvers, Dedham, and Dorchester was built many a sturdy dwelling still standing to show with what solidity these pioneers did their work. In the earliest days of the Colony's struggles too much luxury was not deemed good for those battling with the wilderness. Governor Winthrop writes with some gratification in 1630 of the burning up of some fine table linen, brought by a "godly woman of the Church of Boston" from London, and of which she was very proud.

"But it pleased God that the loss of this linen did her much good, both in taking off her heart from worldly comforts, and in preparing her for a far greater affliction by the untimely death of her husband, who was slain not long after at Isle of Providence."

Yet in 1647, when he married the widow Coytemore, he seems to have had no hesitation in accepting with her a rich dowry, her share of the estate of her former husband, and valued at £640 1s 8d. Among the items were such frivolities as "a silver girdle and a silk iacket." There must have been also other choice garments in the many chests and trunks enumerated. One of these chests is specified as "spruce." The widow had a brave stock of pewter, worth £135, and among other goods unusual at this period were:

Rush-Bottomed Chairs

"1 chest of drawers £1
a copp. furnace £1 10s.
A parcel of cheney platters and soucers £1
2 flaskets
A bedstead, trundle bed with ropes and mats."

It is a matter of wonder how the governor reconciled his conscience to the silver girdle and "iacket," for in 1634 the Massachusetts General Court had particularly prohibited the wearing of either "gold or silver girdles, hattbands, belts, ruffs, and beaver hatts." Also they forbade the purchase of "any appell, either wollen, silke, or lynnen with any lace on it, silver golde, silke or threed." They were only allowed one "slash" on each sleeve and one on the back.

These rules were operative for many years, for in Salem, in 1653, a man is haled before the court for excess "in bootes, rebonds, gould, and silver lace." In Newbury, Mass., in 1653, two women were brought before the court for wearing "a silk hood and scarfe," but both were discharged for proving their husbands were worth over £100. John Hutchin's wife was also discharged "upon testimony of her being brought up above the ordinary ranke." These items show that both rank and property were saving grace even among the Puritans, and no doubt Mrs. Winthrop escaped censure under this rule.

Boston, about 1650, had houses partly of brick and partly of stone, as well as plainer wooden ones. In 1640 John Davys built for William Rix, a weaver, a house "16 feet long and 14 feet wide, with a chamber floare finished with summer and ioysts." There was also a cellar, the walls were covered with clapboards, and the chimney was made of hewn timber, daubed. The whole house cost £21. This was a typical house of a workingman, and must have required little furniture besides the loom to fill it. The fine houses with ample halls and large rooms were but the forerunners of that comfortable style we call by the name Colonial. But they were precious things when once built, and it is by no means uncommon to find them parcelled out to different relatives. In 1658 John Greene of Warwick, R. I., gives to his beloved wife—

—"a large hall and chimni with a little chamber adjoining to the hall, as also a large chamber with a little chamber within y^t, with a large garret and with a little dary room which buttes against ye oule house during her life; also half ye orchard."

Connecticut Chest

It seems as if this bequest might have been open to different interpretations among the heirs. He does not specify if he left the "goods" which were in the hall and rooms,—quite important items.

The widow Francis Killburn's house at Hartford, whose estate in 1650 was valued at £349, had in her hall "tables, formes, chaires, stools, and benches," all valued at £1.

Mr. Palfrey says in his "History of New England" that Whitfield's house at Guilford, Mass., built in 1639, is the oldest house standing now in New England.

There were three stone houses built at Guilford this same year, and it is now asserted that there are quite a number of houses still standing which were built before that of Whitfield. The Barker house at Pembroke, Mass., built in 1628, is said to be the most ancient.

The walls of the Whitfield house are of stone; it is two stories high with garret, and the timber is oak. There are two secret closets which were found by removing a board in the attic. This house was ample and commodious, and the household furnishings were of corresponding value.

In the colonies during the seventeenth century the doublet was worn by women as well as by men. Men wore it over a sleeved waistcoat. The sleeves were elaborately slashed and embroidered. There were falling bands at the neck for those who wished, while the sedately inclined wore white linen collars. Trunk hose were used, and shoes plainly tied or with rosettes. A beaver or felt hat was a necessary adjunct, and all those who could afford it wore gloves, embroidered if possible. These gloves had gauntlets, worked or fringed, and such an important item of dress were the gloves that in 1645 the glovers petitioned the Council to prevent the export of undressed goat-skins.

In many inventories the item of leather breeches appears, and in connection with them the comment "half wore out." Henry Webb, of Boston, who died in 1660, left an estate much of which descended to Harvard College. His wearing-apparel was unusually limited for a man of means. In women's inventories the most important item is always linen or plate, a "ring with a diamond" valued at eight shillings being an unusual piece of luxury belonging to Mistress Anne Hibbins in 1656.

The best articles which New England exported, and for which England was most greedy, were masts, thirty-three to thirty-five inches in diameter, selling for from £95 to £115 each. These and salt fish proved of more value to the colonies than any other commodity possessed at that time.

Much of the furniture of the old homes has disappeared. Some is still retained by the descendants of its original owners, and there are other pieces now gathered in museums, nearly every city endeavouring to retain the mementos of her early history.

By 1700 Philadelphia was quite a flourishing town. The life of the country magnates was elegant and dignified. Many rich men had both town and country houses complete in every detail. Before the Pennsylvania Colony was five years old, (the grant was given March 24, 1681) William Penn had set the example of having a town and country house, the latter being completed in 1685. He owned a coach and a calash, and had, besides, a fine barge with oars-men who rowed him between his house and Philadelphia. Fairfield, the home of the Norris family, was finished in 1717, and was at that time the most beautiful home in Philadelphia. The sashes for the windows and most of the interior woodwork was imported from England, as was the furniture.

The hall was considered wonderfully elegant, being paved with marble. There were substantial houses of brick, the latter of which were home-made, and many artizans of all trades, Dutch as well as English, were coming over. William Penn wrote to his agent of such a one, and said that he was to be set to work making wainscot and tables and chairs, as Penn himself was to bring much furniture with him.

His house in Bucks County was of brick, two stories and a half high, and was comfortably filled with furniture, some, as we see, made before he arrived, but most of which he brought with him. There was much silver plate, pewter dishes, cisterns, etc., beds, tables, stands and chairs. In the best parlour were two tables, one great cane chair, four small cane chairs, one couch, and many cushions of divers materials. The great hall where they dined had "one long table, two forms, and six chairs." The dining-room was a later development, and not until the eighteenth century was well advanced do we find rooms so called in even the better class of houses.

Mahogany Desk

We also see depicted an oak table, of what is called the thousand-legged pattern. It has had an interesting history. It is circular in shape, five feet in diameter, and is in good order. It is said to be part of the furniture brought to America by William Penn, from whom it descended to the Bradfords, a well-known Philadelphia family of printers. It was given by them to a young clerk in their office, named McGowan. In 1849 it came into the possession of Mrs. Oliver's father, and when he died he bequeathed it to his son, Dr. John Hepburn, of Warren, Pa., who gave it to his sister, Mrs. Oliver.

This style of table dates to the first half of the seventeenth century, as may be seen by the drawer which all these early tables had. The brass handle is a late addition, and the drawer has about it the overlapping edge, this style immediately succeeding the drawers with mouldings like those shown in the chest on frame in the first chapter. The legs fold together, fitting into the lower braces, and the leaves drop.

This make of table was always considered of value, so we find them selling at Philadelphia in 1705 at £2; at Boston, 1699, at £2; in 1690 at Salem, "a round, black walnut table, £2 5s." Such a table as this was used by Sir William Johnson, so potent a factor in the settlement of the Mohawk Valley. His table is of mahogany, the leaves drop on hinges, and it has one more leg on each side than our example. It is oval in shape instead of round, six feet six inches long, and five feet eleven inches in its shortest diameter. In 1776 this table was confiscated, and was

76

bought by the Hon. John Taylor. His descendants have lent it to the Albany Historical Society.

The social life in Philadelphia in Revolutionary times was easy and agreeable, consisting of the original Quaker families and another class connected with the government, and these two gave the tone to society. The pleasures of the table were the only luxuries which the sedate Quakers allowed themselves, and the city was famous for the quality of its Madeira and French wines, and the wonderful cooking of West India turtle. In 1778 differences in rank were strongly marked. The labourer wore his leather breeches, checkered shirt, and neat's-hide shoes. The queue or club was still worn by men of fashion; so were rich broadcloth coats of every colour except scarlet, which was seen only on the "backs of soldiers, Carolinians, and dancing-masters." Winthrop Sargent, a Philadelphian himself, writing of this time, says:

"Silver tankards and china punch-bowls were evidences of prosperity, as were the small mirrors in wooden frames, and the mahogany tea-boards that are still sometimes met with in the lumber-rooms of old-time houses. Glass tumblers were rarely seen, a dipper for the punch-bowl, or gourd or cup for the water-pail supplied those who did not have recourse to the vessel itself."

This latter statement seems hardly compatible with "elegance," but there were certainly great extremes to be met with even in the Capitol City, as Philadelphia was at that time.

When it became fashionable to have tables round or oval, it was no longer possible to use forms or settles at them. So chairs took their place, and we

Corner Cupboard

notice with greater frequency in the inventories "sets" of chairs, six, twelve, and occasionally twenty-four. These early chairs, straight-backed with rush or bass bottoms, or of carved wood or leather, were hard to sit upon, so cushions were provided in large numbers and of varying degrees of elegance. These rush-bottomed chairs with turned wood frames remained in use for many years. They were made with different degrees of elaboration, one of the two in showing a more ornamental banister back (*i. e.*, the vertical slats) than the other. These two chairs have seen much service, but are uncommonly well preserved, and belong to Mr. William M. Hoyt, of Rochester, N. Y. They were frequently painted dark green, a fashion said to have come to us from Holland. As chairs grew more comfortable the decrease in the number of cushions is very marked.

With the increase in comfort in household belongings a corresponding increase in the elegance of dress was visible. There was a "court circle" in America as well

77

as in England. Broadway, as early as 1700, presented a brilliant sight at church time. Lord Bellomont was governor, and Colonel Bayard and his wife were citizens of wealth and importance. On such an occasion as church-going, on a fine spring morning, Mrs. Bayard wore no bonnet, but a "frontage", a sort of head-dress of rows of muslin stiffened with wire. She also wore a "steenkirk", or voluminous necktie, which fell over her bodice. The skirt of her purple and gold atlas gown was cut away to show her black velvet petticoat edged with two silver orrices, and short enough to show her green silk stockings and fine embroidered shoes. Her hair was powdered and her kerchief scented with rosewater.

The furniture in use at this time has been already shown in Chapter I. Oak chairs, leather chairs, and those of cane are all mentioned. We find entries of "12 cane chairs with black frames" (1712); "6 Spanish leather chairs" (1703); "one fine chest of drawers," of maple (1703); "a fine chest of drawers of olive and walnut wood" (1705) and other similar items.

Furniture was now being made in the Colonies in quite large quantities, and New England was actively engaged in the furniture business, which employed many cabinet-makers. Salem had James Symond as early as 1714, and others, with each succeeding year. Lynn had John Davis by 1703,

Banquet Room, Independence Hall, Philadelphia

and Marblehead, which was expected to become a great commercial centre, had at least a dozen more or less celebrated between 1729 and 1780. The Connecticut chest is an example of home-made furniture. It is known to collectors as the Connecticut chest, because this design is found only in that vicinity. Quite a number of such chests are in existance, all bearing the same pattern carved on the panels. They are of oak, often with pine tops, backs, and bottoms. The one shown has the top of oak; the turned drops and ornaments are of pine stained black; its height is 40 inches, width 48 inches, and breadth 22 inches. It is at Deerfield, Mass.

In the eighteenth century ministers were often glad to turn their hands to some work which would eke out their slender stipends. We have seen how Mr. Ripley of Concord increased his. The Rev. Theophilus Pickering, of Salem, in 1724, made furniture. Pieces are still in existance which he made, sturdy and in good order,

78

showing that he put his best work and best wood into this business, as he put his best thought into his pulpit labour.

The woods used by these cabinet-makers embrace all kinds, walnut, maple, cherry, nut-wood (hickory), poplar, ash, and pine. American dealers imported mahogany also in quantities, and it was for sale in planks as well as made up into furniture.

"New York Gazette and Weekly Mercury" for 1774 published the following advertisements.

"To be sold by Leonard Kip, A quantity of New Beef by the barrel, Honey by the barrel or half barrel, Albany boards and planks, Highland butter in firkins and European Goods. Which he will sell very low for cash or short credit, at his store in Dock Street opposite Mr. Gerardus Duyckinck's."

The following also appeared in many issues of the paper.

"Mahogany Furniture, 3 elegant desks & book cases, 1 chest upon chest of drawers, 1 lady's dressing-chest & bookcase, 3 desks & 1 pr. card tables, 2 setts of chairs, 3 dining-tables & 5 breakfast tables, 1 clock-case furnished with a good plain 8 day clock, Sundry stands, etc. The above articles are well made and most of them are of wood of the first quality and will be sold as low as any furniture of equal value in the city by Willett & Pearsey, cabinet & chair-makers, at the sign of the clothes-press nearly opposite the Oswego Market, at the end of Maiden Lane."

In Philadelphia, renowned for its manufacture of household goods, the trade was so large and important that the "Journeyman's Cabinet & Chair-maker's Philadelphia Book of Prices" was issued. In a second edition (1795) are given the prices of many local furniture-makers, such as:

"A plain mahogany high-post bedstead £1. 4s. 6d.

"A plain sofa 6 ft. long, with 6 legs, fast back & no low rails. £1. 8s. 0d."

The mahogany desk pictured is a piece found at Bedford Springs, Pa., a place which was known as a "resort" as early as 1778, and had houses with plastered walls, quite an unusual luxury in country regions, though as these Springs were frequented by the fashionable society of Philadelphia and New York, who went for the waters, special effort was used to make the place attractive. The desk is mahogany and solid, not veneered. It has a roll-top of the style made by Sheraton, which falls back behind the drawers and cupboards.

The brasses are new, and the lid has been restored; otherwise the desk is as it was made. It stood for many years in one of the little outside houses near the main hotel, and when, a number of years ago, a visitor asked to buy it, the proprietor told him the piece was known as "Jimmy Buchanan's desk." Mr. Buchanan was in the habit of spending his summers at Bedford Springs and always occupied the room where this desk was. In 1857, when as President Buchanan he arrived at Bedford, the proprietors in his honour had refurnished his room.

They were congratulating themselves that the President would be gratified at what they had done for him, when he suddenly came into the room and demanded in a rage what had become of the desk. If it was not forthcoming he would go elsewhere. He could use it, he said, to write on, and then the drawers were roomy and just suited him for his clean shirts. It is needless to say that the desk was brought down from the garret, and was never removed from the room when President Buchanan visited there.

Windsor Chairs

The desk is in company suited to its age, the larger powder-horn hanging above it being a veteran also. It is seventeen inches long and ten inches broad at the largest end. It bears the following inscription cut in quaint old letters on lines drawn so that they should go straight:

"This is William Norton's Horn made at Qubeck ye 10 day of Aprill 1776. I powder with my Brother Ball we wound them all that in Our way may chance to fall."

The smaller horn bears the date 1810, and the two swords were used in the General Training days of the first quarter of the nineteenth century. All these relics belong to Anthony Killgore, Esq., of Flemington, N. J.

During the first quarter of the eighteenth century, and even a little earlier, houses were built with wainscoting and panelling, and it was the fashion to build into walls cupboards for the display of china and plate. Frequently they were placed in the corner of the room, and were either with or without doors. Such a cupboard was called a "beaufait," which was sometimes shortened to "bofet," or "buffet," according to the taste of the owner. A specimen of said corner cupboard is pictured earlier.

The house from which this beaufait came was built in 1696 in Vernon Place, Boston, Mass., by William Clough. Two years later he sold it, and it passed through several hands by inheritance and sale till in 1758 it was bought by Captain Vernon, who with various members of his family held it for seventy-five years. The cherub's heads which ornament the cupboard are somewhat unusual on a piece of furniture of this kind, and it has also a very handsome shell at the top. It is now at the Old State House, Boston.

Mention is also made in many inventories of "Court cupboards," and "livery cupboards." The former were light movable shelves, making a kind of sideboard, and used to display plate and porcelain. A livery cupboard was somewhat similar. It had usually but three shelves and stood upon four legs. It sometimes had a drawer for linen, but no doors. Mugs and cups were hung from the bottom of the shelves, and a ewer stood below. These were put in what was called the dining-parlour, a stately room on the second floor never used to dine in.

The picture earlier shows the banquet room at Independence Hall, Philadelphia, with the beautiful moulding, wainscot, and over-mantel which were seen in handsome houses in the middle of the eighteenth century.) It was many years before the dining-room was set apart for meals. At first only a screen gave privacy, but gradually the dining-room grew in favour. The early dining-rooms held beds, as well as the parlours, they being given to guests on account of the warmth. Joint stools were there, and Flanders chests, in which the mistress often rummaged, so that the guest should see the goodly store of clothes and linen owned by the family.

As was the custom in England, many wealthy men had their furniture made to order, often in their own houses, where the cabinet-makers came and worked. Sometimes they imported their own woods, as in the case of Mr. Champlin, a merchant of Newport, R. I., who brought home with him in 1762, from a voyage in the West Indies, some logs of mahogany, from which he had several pieces of furniture made. Watson, in his "Annals of New York," says that the use of what was foreign and modish was noted earlier in New York before the Revolution than elsewhere.

"They earlier used carpets, wall-papers, foreign milliners, dress-makers, Windsor chairs, glass utensils, jewelry, dentistry, watches, umbrellas, stage-playbills, etc.

Windsor chairs were advertised in 1768 as made and sold by William Gautier in New

Wallpaper

York. He also had high-backed, low-backed, sack-backed chairs and settees, and dining and low chairs. A pair of Windsor chairs are shown on the previous page.

Carriages were imported in 1766 from Dublin, as also men to keep them in repair. They were landaus, curricles, sedans, and even sleighs with gildings, carvings, and japan to suit. In 1774 there was advertised for sale "A handsome Riding Chair with full set of harness," and an announcement was made that there was "To be sold a Genteel Post-chaise."

The carpets referred to above were imported ones, Turkey and Scotch. "Persian and plat carpeting" was offered for sale in 1761 by H. Van Vleck. A later advertisement announced: "There will be sold at Public Auction, April 7, 1777, Two very handsome Turkey carpets." Rag carpets were used as early as 1660, and

81

private families who could afford it owned their own looms. Sometimes those who wished extra elegance bought the yarn and paid for the weaving.

In 1761, "Pennsylvania Stoves newly invented, both round and square, to be sold by Peter Clopper" were advertised in the "New York Gazette." These were, no doubt, what became known as Franklin stoves. This same year were also advertised wall-papers by quite a number of firms in various cities: "A variety of paper-hangings imported from London." "Flowered papers," "printed papers," and "printed papers for hanging rooms," were imported as early as 1752. The image above shows the fashionable wallpaper of about this period. It is in the Cowles House, Deerfield, Mass., and is in an excellent state of preservation. The sofa below is of the late Sheraton or early Empire, similar to the one belonging to Rev. Mr. Ripley and shown in the respective chapter. Some wall-paper of equal elaboration is shown in the Frontispiece, which gives the hallway of the famous "King Hooper House," built at Danvers, Massachusetts.

Wall-paper, however, was not very generally used,—just why one cannot tell, but some of the gaily flowered papers were used for window-shades. Curtains for windows and beds were at this time very popular, and it was the fashion of the time to have the window- and bed-curtains alike. The materials were very numerous and their names have a most unfamiliar sound. There was perpetuana, Kitterminster, serge, darnick (a coarse damask,) silke darnick, camlet, mohair, fustian, seersucker, camac or camoca, bancour, red and green paly-(vertical stripes of equal size,) printed calico, checked and striped linen, India and Patma chintzes, corded dimities, harrateen, lutestring, moreens of all colours, fine French chintzes, Pompadour chintzes, "fine laylock and fancy callicoes," and "muzlins." There were bed-cords, and fringes to edge and trim all these materials, and the bed in full dress was a very ornamental affair.

Beds varied in size and height in quite a remarkable degree. The one shown on the following page has a very wide reputation, and is now to be seen at the rooms of the Antiquarian Society, Concord, Mass. It is of

Bed at Concord, Massachusetts

mahogany, with bandy legs and ball-and-claw feet. The curtains are the original ones that came with the bed and are worn in many places. They are very curious showing agricultural scenes and domestic animals in large numbers. These curtains were not intended to be drawn, but to hang permanently in place, and there were to be inner curtains of "muzlin" or "callico" to draw and keep out drafts. One peculiarity of this bed is its extreme narrowness; it is intended for a double bed and yet its width is only four feet, it was included in the wedding outfit of Miss Martha Tufts, who was married at Concord in 1774. The cabriole leg and style of curtain lead to the supposition that the piece is Dutch.

In February, 1768, Miss Harriott Pinckney was married to Daniel Horry in "Charles Town," South Carolina. This was one of twelve weddings that took place that year, all the bridegrooms being wealthy rice-planters. The furniture to fill the houses of these rich couples was all brought from England, and the beds were lofty mahogany ones, four-posters with tester, canopy, curtains, and valances complete. The large heavy posts for all twelve beds were said to be alike, and were carved with rice-stalks, the heavy clustering heads forming the capitals. So tall were these beds that steps were necessary to climb into them, and the ones belonging to Mrs. Horry were in existence a few years ago.

In the "History and Present State of Virginia," 1705, is the following paragraph relating to the homes:

"The private buildings are of late very much improved; several Gentlemen having built themselves large Brick Houses of many Rooms on a floor and several stories high, as also some Stone-Houses; but they don't covet to make them lofty having extent enough of Ground to build upon. They always contrive to have large rooms that they may be cool in Summer. Of late they have made their Stories much higher than formerly, and their windows large and sasht with Cristal Glass, and within they adorn their apartments with rich furniture."

The eighteenth century was rightly called the Golden Age of Virginia. The planter in his manor-house, surrounded by his family, served by a vast army of retainers, was like a feudal patriarch, though his rule was milder. On the plantation itself were produced all the necessaries of

Bed at Mount Vernon

life; it was a little community in itself. Wool was woven into clothing, flax was spun, shoes were made, and blacksmithing done. Luxuries such as books, wines, silks, laces, and the more elegant household plenishings were brought to the very wharf from London in the planters' own ships in return for tobacco. The writer previously quoted goes on to say, about the people themselves:

—"They are such abominable ill husbands that, though their country be overrun with wood, yet they have all their wooden ware from England, their cabinets, chairs, tables, stools, chests, boxes, cart-wheels, and all other things, even so much as their bowls and birchen brooms, to the eternal reproach of their laziness."

Although Beverly calls himself an "Inhabitant of Virginia", it is curious that he was not aware that the southern colonies were interdicted by special act of legislature from trading with the Dutch or English colonies. "Wooden ware" is especially mentioned as being subject to "imposicon."

A typical bed of the last quarter of the eighteenth century is shown above This bed belonged to George Washington, and is in his bedroom at Mount Vernon. It is said to be the one he used in his last illness. Unlike the bed shown on the previous page, this bed is of unusual proportions, being nearly as wide as it is long. The small table between the doors shows an excellent example of the Dutch foot. Upon it stands a small dressing-glass, so much in use at this period, of very handsome black and gold lacquer. Whenever General Washington had the opportunity he added to the furniture and appointments of Mount Vernon. Belvoir, the home of the Fairfax family, was one of the most splendid of the mansions on the Potomac. In 1774 its contents were sold at auction, and Colonel George Washington bought goods to the value of £200 sterling. Among the most important lots were the following:

"1 mahogany shaving desk, 1 settee bed and furniture (£13), 4 mahogany chairs, 1 chamber carpet, 1 oval glass with gilt frame, 1 mahogany chest and drawers in Mrs. Fairfax's chamber, (£12. 10s) 1 mahogany sideboard, (£12. 5s.) 1 mahogany cistern and stand, 1 mahogany voider, 1 desk and 1 knife tray, 12 chairs & 3 window curtains from dining room (£31), 1 mahogany wash desk, (£1. 2s. 6d.)."

Among the smaller articles were several pairs of andirons, tongs and shovels, bellows, brushes, toasting-forks, and "1 hot rache in cellar," with many blankets, 19 coverlids, pillows, bolsters, bottles and pickle-pots, wine-glasses and pewter water-plates. There were also two tables, one "a mahogany spider-make tea-table, £1 11s." and "1 mahogany table £11," showing that articles of this wood obtained good values even then. The list of the goods in all of the rooms of Belvoir is far too long to be given here, but in the dressing-room connected with Colonel Fairfax's bedroom were "1 oval glass in burnished gold, (£5 10s.), 1 mahogany shaving-table, 1 mahogany desk (£16 16s.), 4 chairs and covers, 1 mahogany settee bedstead, Saxon green, covers for same, 1 mahogany Pembroke table, dogs, shovel, tongs and fender."

It is also a matter of interest to see of what books a library consisted among people who were considered to have a literary bent and to be extensive readers. There is nothing "light" about it, and would to-day be accounted very dull reading.

Batavia Illustrated
A New Body of Geography
London Magazine, 7 vols.
Croope's Law Reports
Parkinson's Herbal
Heylin's Cosmography, in 4 vols.
Knoll's History of the Turkish Empire
Collection of Voyages and Travels
Coke's Institutes of the Laws of England, 3 vol. Political Discourses by Henry, Earl of Monmouth
England's Recovery
Wooten's State of Christendom
Laws of the Colony of Massachusetts Bay
Hobart's Law Reports
Laws of Merchants
Johnson's Excellency or Monarchical Government
Laws of Virginia Latin and French Dictionary
Complete Clerk and Conveyancer
Langley's Pomona, or Gardening
Hawkin's Pleas of the Crown
A Political Piece

Gunnel's Offences of the Realm of England
Strada's History of the Low Country Wars
Ainsworth's
English and Latin Dictionary
Spanish and English Dictionary
Haine's Dictionary of Arts and Sciences
Latin Bible
Blackmore's Prince Arthur A Poem on Death
History of the Twelve Cæsars by Suetonius
Judgement & Hell
John Calvin's Institution of Religion
Knox's Martyrology
Fuller's Church History from its Rise
Jacob's Law Dictionary
Locke on the Human Understanding
Chamberlayne's Great Britain
Hughes's Natural History of Barbadoes
Laws of His Majesty's Plantations.

A bed showing better the handsome solid posts is given in the image above. This is also associated with the Father of his Country, for it is in the house at Somerville, N. J., occupied by him as headquarters during one of his campaigns in the Revolutionary War.

In Chapter I a "bedsteade of carven oak" was referred to as having

Bed at Somerville, New Jersey

been sent for to England by Mrs. Lake, as a wedding-present for her daughter. It could hardly have been such a very splendid piece of furniture as the image shortly to follow, with its coat of arms on the headboard, and the two beautiful foot-posts.

The draperies were intended to cover the two head-posts, so that they were left plain. The old easy-chair standing beside the bed has unfortunately lost its feet, but they were the well-known ball-and-claw pattern generally seen on this style of chair, which was well calculated to keep off swirling draughts from the head and back of the occupant. These chairs were popular for a century or more, and were made not only by English cabinet-makers like Chippendale and Hepplewhite, but by the Dutch and Flemish makers as well. They all have the bandy leg, but the Dutch foot is sometimes used instead of the ball-and-claw.

But all the luxury and elegance were not absorbed by the South and New York. Boston kept well to the front. In 1700 Andrew Faneuil, Huguenot, came to Boston and engaged in business. His brother was in this country, too, and, he dying not long after, Andrew assumed the care of, and took into business with himself, first one and then a second nephew. They were merchants and the following entries of consignments, taken from their old ledgers, which are still in existence, show the nature of their business. Besides crapes, poplins, lawns, and silks, they had for sale durants and duroys, osnaburgs, camblets, narrow, double and cherry, with ingrains, silk druggets and calamancoes. They also imported dishes, pans, and kettles, "wooden lanthorns and tin ditto" (1725). Nor did they neglect to provide amusement for their fellow townsmen, for they imported "one-half gross man-in-the-moon cards." Among other goods in this same invoice were "1 chest muskets and one large pair looking-glasses."

Andrew Faneuil died in 1738, and his favourite nephew and chief heir, Peter Faneuil, did not hesitate, on account of the cost, to have an elaborate and seemly funeral. Three thousand pairs of gloves were distributed, and later two hundred mourning-rings were given to intimate friends. Peter Faneuil, now a wealthy young man by inheritance as well as by his own exertions, lived in the old house with his maiden sister. This same year, 1738, he sends to London for "a handsome chariot with two setts of harness,"

Carved Oak Bedstead

and a coachman warranted to remain sober. A few months later he writes for china and glass from England, for table-cloths and napkins from France, and he sends for

86

silver spoons, "forks with three prongs," all to have upon them the Faneuil crest. "Let them be very neat and handsome," says he.

The next order is for silver candlesticks and a punch-bowl of silver holding two gallons, also to be decorated with the family crest. His clothes were also a matter of concern, and he sends to London a pattern of a piece of Duncy, orders buttons of the newest fashion to match it, of mohair silk, and knee-straps. Nor is he less scrupulous about his sister's affairs, and sent all the way back to London six pairs of stockings which had been sent of worsted instead of "3 pairs thread hose, and 1 pair Galous hose, and 2 pair of thread ditto."

Boston at this time (1738) seems to have had some luxuries demanded by New York, for an order comes to Peter Faneuil to send there "a dozen red Turkey or Morocker leather chairs." One of these easy-chairs cost £14 14*s*. In 1742 Peter Faneuil gave to the city of Boston the hall called by his name. It was built of home-made brick (Salem had a brick-kiln as early as 1629), but the glass in the windows was brought from England in Mr. Faneuil's own ships. The first furnishings bought by the selectmen for Faneuil Hall were "two pairs of brass candlesticks with steel snuffers, and a poker, for the town's use."

Peter Faneuil's inventory, filed in 1742, contains items under 158 heads, and makes quite a volume of manuscript. It includes not only his and his uncle's gatherings in the way of household goods, but the contents of warehouses, cellar, coach-house, and stables. The house was handsomely furnished. In the best room were, "12 carved vineered chairs & couch, £105; 1 pier glass, £100." Other costly articles were, "1 buffet with parcel of china delph & glass, £199." There were, besides,—

—"1 chimney glass and arms; 1 marble table; 1 large Turkey carpet; 1 compleat brass sett, hearth-dogs, tongs, shovel, and bellows; 1 copper tea-table; cups, saucers, tea-pot, stand, bowl and sugar-dish; 3 alabaster bowls and stands; 1 large oval mahogany table, 12 plain walnut-frame leather-bottom chairs; 1 prospect of Boston, 2 landskips on copper, and the Temple of Solomon."

The "Great Centre Hall" must have made a quaint appearance, since here hung the fire apparatus; "1 large entry lantern; 12 baggs and buckets, and books £50."

The sleeping-rooms were handsomely equipped, and each was furnished with its appropriate colour. The list includes:

"1 harrateen bed, bedstead and window curtains, matrass and two green silk quilts and feather-bed, £65

3 scones with arms

1 bureau, 1 table, 1 pr. brass-faced dogs, 1 fire-shovel, tongs bellows, and one Turkey carpet, £107"

Peter Faneuil's own room was not lacking in comforts, as is shown by the enumeration of:

—"1 silver-hilted sword, 1 pair of pistols and 1 powder-flask, £15; 1 case 6 razors, bone penknife, strap, 2 bottles, looking-glass tipt with silver; yellow mohair bed-counterpane, feather-bed, bolster, 2 false pillows, false curtains, 6 chairs, 1 great chair, 2 stools, window curtains," etc.

The furnishings of this room, exclusive of the small-arms, was valued at £245. He had "6 lignum-vitæ chocolate-cups lined with silver", which were probably Dutch, for among the goods of Sara Van der Vulgen, of Schenectady, at about this same period, was a great "saler" or salt-cellar, made of lignum-vitæ, bound with silver and standing on three little silver feet.

In Mr. Faneuil's kitchen were many utensils of copper, pots, pans, and kettles, together with an "engine and cistern." He had many jewels, 1,400 ounces of plate, including a shaving-basin worth £40. There were silver snuff-boxes, seven gold rings, and "chrystall buttons set in gold." Just before he died he sent to London for "six gross of the very best London King Henry's cards", for his store no doubt, for cards were becoming more popular among the descendants of the Puritans than they had been.

In 1729 Governor Burnet, of New York and Massachusetts, died, leaving behind him a long list of valuable personal goods. He owned as many as seventy chairs and twelve tables. The chairs were of mahogany and walnut, with leather or bass bottoms, and one easy-chair was covered with silk. Twenty-four chairs had seats of red leather, a noble set, and there are two chairs now in the Yale University Library which belonged to Governor Burnet, and which are of the exact style of what we call Chippendale. They were made more than twenty-five years before the "Director" was published, but are made of mahogany with richly carved knees, ball-and-claw feet, with carved and ornamentally pierced splats, handsome upper rail curved and ending in the little ears before mentioned.

In all the inventories of wealthy and poor alike there is mention of candlesticks, sconces, girandoles, etc. The "entry lanthorns," as well as the perforated tin ones, were made to hold bits of candles and lamps are few and far between. It was not till 1783 that the flat-wick lamp was invented, the lamps before that time being pewter and glass, with small, round, string wicks, burning whale oil. When the question of lighting was so difficult, it is no wonder that the pioneers were in the habit of going to bed at dark and rising with the sun. The bayberry or candleberry was of recognized value, and the laws of Brookhaven, as early as 1687, forbade the gathering of the berries before September 15, under a penalty of a fine of fifteen shillings.

Candlewood, as pine knots were called, was burned in the fireplace on long winter evenings. The manufacture of home-made candles was one of the tests by which the careful housewife was distinguished, dozens of candles being made and laid away in the candle-box. In 1753, in the "New York Gazette," were advertised "Green mould candles for sale, at the Old Slip Market." The old moulds, generally of tin, were passed around among neighbours in country districts and villages. "Dipping" candles was a trying business, and required skill and experience on the part of the dipper. Lustres holding many candles were used on festive occasions, and four or six lights were often set in branches on either side of mirrors. Many candlesticks with cut-glass prisms are still to be found, and betty-lamps, crude little metal lamps, were often used for bedrooms or in sick-rooms. "Glass lamps and chamber lamps" were advertised as early as 1759, and "fine large lamps at 20 shilling each" in 1752. Candle-screens, "red, green, gilt and black japanned candlesticks with snuffers and extinguishers", were on sale in 1773, and no card-table was complete without at least a pair of tall massive candlesticks of Sheffield plate.

By 1760 the newspapers contain advertisements of what are really luxuries. James Gilliland, dealer in earthen, delf, and glass in Wall street, New York, has the following named articles: "Enamelled and cabbage teapots [Wedgwood, no doubt], cut and ground glass decanters, tumblers, punch and wine glasses."

The fair sex is by no means forgotten, and even during the stress of the great struggle for freedom her appearance is considered. Many times the following announcement appears: "The Venetian Paste so well-known to the ladies for enameling the Hands, neck and face of a lovely white" is for sale by Hugh Gaine, printer. Nesbit Deane offers hats "to exceed in fineness, cut, colour, and cock." He also has "Ladies' white riding hats." "Goods for the approaching season" are duly set forth in the spring advertisements, and "Sagothies, Hairbine, white silk embroidered and tambour with gold shades" are recommended for waistcoats. There was also to be bought "gold and silver vellum lace, gold and silver bullion fringe, silk sashes and hat feathers for the gentlemen of the militia and army." "Spittlefield corded tabbey, peneaffcoes and peling sattens" were to be had in all colours for ladies' use, while "Prunells and Oxford crape" were provided for the "Rev'd clergy."

The servant question was a burning issue even at that time, and there are quantities of rewards offered for runaway slaves and apprentices. Some desperate householder advertised in March, 1777:

"WANTED. A cook, black or white, male or female. Such a person will meet with good encouragement by applying to Hugh Gaine, printer."

Those who did not wish to be annoyed by the labour of housekeeping could be accommodated with "Diet and Lodging," also, by applying to Hugh Gaine, printer.

Other advertisements read:

[1761] "Morrison, peruke maker from London, dresses ladies and gentlemen's hair in the politest taste. He has a choice parcel of human, horse, and goat's hairs to dispose of."

[1768] "James Daniel, wig-maker and hairdresser also operates on the teeth, a business so necessary in this city."

Wigs were an important feature in the costume of the men. They were subject to tax and were a good source of revenue. The Treasurer of the Colony of New York, as early as 1732, reported that he had received from the tax on wigs the sum of £9 17s. 6d. This tax was called—

—"a wise and prudent measure, because it was the fashion for even young boys to conceal their own hair under large and spacious wigs. To repress a custom so absurd, or to make a source of revenue has been the object of the legislature."

So we paid, and gladly, for our wigs, even though visiting Englishmen spoke of us thus: "The people, both in town and country, are sober, industrious, and hospitable, though intent upon gain."

All travellers mention our hospitality. Prince de Broglie writes in 1782:

"M. de la Luzerne took me to tea at Mrs. Morris, wife of the Secretary of the Treasury of the United States. Her house is small, but well ordered and neat, the doors and tables of superb well-polished mahogany, the locks and andirons of polished brass, the cups arranged symetrically, the mistress of the house good-looking and very grey."

Mrs. Morris was considered to have one of the handsomest houses in Philadelphia, and it was not at all the mode to display one's own hair if it had turned grey, so the fact of Mrs. Morris doing so seems to have impressed the volatile Frenchman.

Another traveller, Captain Laurence Butler, writes from Westmoreland, Virginia, in 1784, to Mrs. Craddock, an Englishwoman, as follows:

Late colonial era Highboy chest of drawers - Image: Forever Wiser

"When balls are given, which is very frequent, the company stay all night (not as in your country), for every gentleman has ten or fifteen beds, which is sufficient for the ladies, and the men shift for themselves."

These beds were the high four-posters, carved and draped, and ten or fifteen seems a liberal allowance for every household. One Alexander Mackraby, visiting Philadelphia in 1768, before the Revolution, writes home: "I could hardly find myself out this morning in a most elegant crimson silk damask bed." Poor indeed was the householder who did not manage to have one "feder bed," or one of flock, or something soft, and there were always pillows, bolster, coverlids, and blankets, though sometimes, judging from the inventories, the owners did not care particularly about sheets.

90

Colonial and Later Periods – Part Two

W E have seen by the middle of the century, 1750, how many comforts were obtainable at the large centres, and how many cabinet-makers were at work in the Colonies. About 1756 the ways and people are described thus:

"New York is one of the most social places on the continent. The men collect themselves into weekly evening clubs. The ladies in winter are frequently entertained either at concerts of musick or assemblies, and make a very good appearance. They are comely and dress well, and scarce any of them have distorted shapes. Tinctured with a Dutch education they manage their families with becoming parsimony, good providence, and singular neatness."

Twenty-five years later the British officers quartered in New York made life there very happy, if controversial. Fox-hunting was practiced till 1781, and was advertised in the "Royal Gazette" as taking place on Ascot Heath, in Brooklyn. Horse-racing took place on Hempstead Plains, Long Island, for life in general was a full copy of what was going on in England. The "New York Gazette" of June 4, 1770, tells us that—

Room in Whipple House, Ipswich Mass.

"...a Great Horse-Race was run off on Hempstead Plains for a considerable wager, which engaged the attention of so many in the city that upward of seventy chairs and chaises were carried over the ferry from hence, and a far greater number of horses, so that it was thought that the number of Horses on the Plains at the Races far exceeded a thousand."

The comparatively peaceful sport of horse-racing was not the only one indulged in. Bull-baiting was not at all unusual. The posters for this amusement were headed "Pro Bono Publico," and in the "New York Mercury" for August, 1774, John Cornell announces that there will be "a Bull Baited on Town Hill at 3 o'clock every

Thursday during the season." Town Hill was Columbia Street, near Cranberry Street, Brooklyn Heights.

On March 24, 1777, in the "New York Mercury" was the following advertisement:

"On Thursday At the Theatre in John St. On next Thursday evening will be performed a Tragedy called Venice Preserved. With an Occasional Prologue. To which will be added a Farce called 'The Lying Valet.' The Characters by the Gentlemen of the Army and Navy."

As for clothes, of course the people followed the English styles, and copies of such magazines as "The Maccaroni Magazine or Monthly Intelligence of the Fashions &

Carved and Gilded Mirror Frame.

Diversions," found their way to America. Here is an extract from the issue October, 1772:

"Hats are rising behind and falling before. The blazing gold loop and full-moon button is now totally exploded, and succeeded by a single narrow looping, broad hatband, and pin's-head button. In full dress the three buttons zigzag with the foretop à la Grecque. Roses are entirely confined to Cheapside, and bags are increasing daily. The late stunting of coats having promoted the growth of skirts, the pockets are capable of holding conveniently a tolerable-sized muslin handkerchief and smelling bottle. Shoes are decreased in heels two inches, and cut like a butter-boat to show the clocks of the stockings."

"The Magazine a la Mode, or Fashionable Miscellany," particularly adapted to the People of both Sexes, and calculated to convey early and useful information to those who are in any way concerned in furnishing articles of Dress, either in "Town or Country," appeared in 1777. From one of these useful repositories we learn under date of 1786 that grass-green was the fashionable colour for gentlemen's suits, that the hair was dressed à la Taureau, and that watch-keys were remarkable for size and weight.

In 1760, pattern-books published in London were to be found in America for the benefit of native cabinet-makers, as the following advertisement duly sets forth:

"John Rivington of Hanover Square has for sale many books for cabinet makers, joiners, etc., and calls particular attention to a new work called Household Furniture for the year 1760, by a society of Upholsterers, Cabinet-makers, etc., containing upwards of 180 Designs consisting of Tea-Tables, Dressing, Card, Writing, Library and Slab tables, Chairs, Stools, Couches, Trays, Chests, Tea-Kettles, Bureaus, Beds, Ornamental Bed Posts, Cornishes, Brackets, Fire-Screens, Desk and Book Cases, Sconces, Chimney-Pieces, Girandoles, Lanthorns, etc., with scales."

Not a paper but had advertisements of furniture offered for sale. Thus in 1774 we find:

"To be sold at private sale a large black walnut cupboard with a set of Delft, a large pier looking-glass, one pair of sconces, 3 large gilt frame pictures, and sundry other articles."

In the same number of the "Weekly Mercury," and in many succeeding issues appears the following notice:

"A scheme for the disposal of a large quantity of silver-plated furniture by lottery. The owner is a Philadelphian."

The image two pages ago shows two looking-glasses of styles that were fashionable about the middle of the eighteenth century.

Mahogany Desk and Chest of Drawers

One of them is dated 1749, of mahogany handsomely carved, and further embellished with [ornaments of chiselled brass, a beading of it being next to the glass. It rests upon two mirror-knobs, which were screwed into the walls to support looking-glasses, and the collection of which is such a pleasing hobby to-day.

The central ornament on the top is missing. The other glass is of carved wood gilded, and is now in Memorial Hall, Philadelphia. It hung for many years in the fine old house "Belmont," and is of the very finest style. The broken-arch cornice is finished with rosettes, and the central ornament is not the usual urn, but something more ornate.

There are constant notices of mahogany for sale, such as:

"A cargo of fine mahogany for sale by Anthony Van Dam, Jan'y 17, 1774."

In May of the same year John Morton advertises—

—"the largest and most elegant assortment of mahogany or gilt oval looking-glass frames ever imported in this city."

William Melbourn advertises also, in 1774, over a hundred items, among them are the following, showing that "small wares" were easily to be obtained:

"White and green ivory table and desert knives and forks.

Ditto with silver caps and ferrils. Ditto black ebony with caps and ferrils. Also Black horn, camwood, centre-bone split buck, sham stag table knives and forks. Carving and oyster knives. Neat mahogany and fish skin knife boxes. Mahogany and fish skin razor cases. Plated coffee pots and spoons. Mahogany tea chests. Merry Andrew, Harry, and Mogul's playing cards, Pearl and ivory fish and counters, Mustard and Marrow spoons."

In Memorial Hall, Philadelphia, is a set of table knives with green ivory handles, like those advertised in the first item, and looking at the end of the blades we can no longer doubt that the use of two-pronged forks was supplemented by a dexterous manipulation of the knife-blades. Writing-desks or scrutoirs, or desks and bookcases, or even desks fitted into the drawers of a bureau, had become pieces of furniture that were found in every well-to-do home.

The image on the previous shows one of the early styles of make, about the middle of the eighteenth century. This particular desk was

Combined Bookcase and Desk

brought from England, is of mahogany, and is in good condition except that the front feet have been restored. It still has the original brasses and the overlapping drawers. It has several secret drawers where during the Revolution the private documents of the owner were concealed. During the Civil War its secret drawers were again in use, and effectually concealed papers of value. It has never passed out of the possession of the family whose ancestors brought it over, and it belongs to Miss Hite, of Waynesboro, Va. The two-drawer chest beside it is of a much earlier period.

The mouldings make the chest part resemble two drawers, but the top opens as is usual. The handles on the desk are of the shape used so much by Hepplewhite on his bureaus and sideboards, while those on the chest are an earlier form of the well-known willow pattern of brasses and are fastened in by wires. The earliest patterns of handles were the knob and drop, which were used on furniture before 1700. These were succeeded by others which were fastened in by wire, and these again were replaced by handles which were affixed with nut and screw. On page 224 are shown the different styles of handles, and their approximate dates. The chest is of mahogany, with bracket foot. This is a most unusual and interesting piece.

At the time of the Revolution there was comfort generally in most of the large cities at least. In 1776 there were sent to Cold Spring, for the use of the army, the following:

"2 Mah'y tables, 6 Rush Bottom chairs, 4 Mah'y Rush Bottoms, and 2 small bedsteads, a kitchen table, a new case of bottles, a Coffee Mill, Brass Scales and Waights, 2 Kitchen Tramels, 2 pickel Tubs and 2 Wash Tubs, an Iron hooped Pail and a soap barrel mostly full of soap and the Ticke of a Stra bed. Value £20."

The works at Cold Spring were destroyed, and the goods were never used, but the Government's strong-box paid for them.

"1 Fether bed Holl'd Tick, 1 Boulster, 1 Pillow,
   1 Coverlin to bed
1 Bedsted 20s.—1 Green Rug 55s.
2 large Rose Blanckets
1 large lookinglass
2 chaina Teapots
8 Burnt China Chocolate Cups
½ Doz Teacups and Saucers
4 tea plates
2 large Cream Couler sauce cups
½ doz blew chaina plates
½ " cream couler "
1 dining-table black cherry wood
1 Teble larg
1 large Copper Kittle
1 Brass Kittle
6 Flat back chairs
1 Holland cubberd neatly adorned with Waxwork
1 Barrel soap
3 Wine Canters
4　　"　　glasses
1 chest wt. Clothing and linen
1　　"　　"　　Sundry books & 1 large Dutch Bible
1 large Kibbe, 1 Sermon book some of the others Divinity & some History
1 New Spinning Weale
12 pictures w't Glass over
1 larg Knot Bowl Cost
2　　"　　"　　"　　"
2 beds with Straw
2 fine worked Baskets
1 Tapend Water Crane

Cornelis Van Santvoordt, who lived at Esopus, near Kingston, N. Y., when it was burned by the British October 16, 1777, put in a claim for damages for £54 17s. 3d. a large variety of goods, as may be seen from the following list:

This inventory is somewhat unusual from the number of "Chaina" articles enumerated, and among all the items there are but six chairs and not a stool. This claim, with many others, is recorded in the "New York Records of the Revolution," and it was paid out of the "strong-box." This box was not a mythical object at all, but a veritable chest. Gerard Bancker was State Treasurer for twenty years. During the

Field Bed

Revolution the iron chest moved about from one place to another like the Continental Congress, and the Treasurer went with it. According to a custom of the times Mr. Bancker took the chest with him when he retired from office. His family kept it for a hundred years, but with many other relics it was sold in Philadelphia, in 1898, by one of his descendants.

Low Four-Post Bed

There were various patterns of combinations of desks and bookcases, and of desks and bureaus. There were the high, wide ones of Chippendale or Sheraton, that would almost fill one side of a room. There were small ones with desk below and shelves above, and occasionally there were such great ones as that shown earlier in this part. This piece of furniture is so tall and massive that it could not have been accommodated in any save a large house. It is over eight feet tall and five feet three inches wide. It is of a light mahogany, with pillars of Empire style and very handsome brasses. The lid of the desk folds back on itself and below it is a drawer and cupboard. The handsomest things about the

96

bookcase are the glass doors with Gothic tracery. The date of this piece is about the first decade of the nineteenth century. The four legs on the front are of unusual elegance. It belongs to the Historical Society at Albany.

Quite as interesting as the inventories of property left by will are some old records in the State Library, New Jersey, called a "Record of the Damages done by the British and their adherents to the Inhabitants of Middlesex Co., New Jersey." This contains the inventories made by six hundred and fifty persons who suffered from the depredations of the plundering Hessians and the English soldiery. The lists extend over the years from 1776 to 1782 inclusive, but the worst mischief was done in the time from December, 1776, to June, 1777. There were eighteen hundred horses taken, and these form a single item. That the settlers were good livers the following inventory of one patriot shows. He lost—

—"4 hogsheads of cider, ½ pipe of madeira, 10 gallons brandy, 7 gallons Jamaica brandy, ½ barrel cherry Rum, barrel Porter."

The inventory does not state his business, but we trust from appearances that he kept a "public."

Another list reads:

"Three cupboards of Dutch make as good as new, also three large Bibles 1 Dutch and 2 English."

David Harriott, of Middlesex County, was completely stripped by the enemy. Among many items were—

"a set of Homespun curtains wove with damask flowers, one

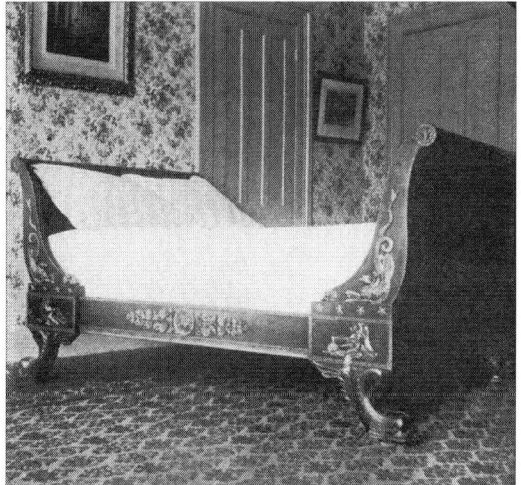

French Bed

ditto of white in large damask flowers, and one ditto of double dimons."

Napkins, quilts, bedspreads, and sheets, as well as large-flowered damask table-cloths and linen covers testify to the industry of the women of the family. The good wife lost her long gowns and short gowns, her "shifts of 500 linen," handkerchiefs of gauze, lawn, and linen, aprons of new flowered lawn, fine linen and homespun, 3 caps of cambric and lawn, all new, and even two bibs for a child. They took all of David's clothes and his silver teaspoons and buckles, smashed his windows and doors, broke down his partitions, drove off his cattle, and did not leave him so much as "a bed, a piggin, a trammel, or a gridiron."

Jacob Hyer was another sufferer. His house must have been one of considerable size and well furnished. There are many items, among them—

97

—"5 fluted brass candlesticks, 2 pr. common ditto, 1 doz. iron ditto, 10 pr. snuffers; 11 feather beds with bolsters and pillows, etc."

The enemy left him nothing, even taking his "Iron chain for Smoke Jack." Much of the furniture listed in these inventories was evidently of American make, for the woods mentioned are bilstead, gum pine, walnut, cherry, or red cedar. The last was the favorite. "Bilstead" was maple.

The beds were chiefly of three styles, field beds, high four-posters with testers and valance, and low four-posters, with an occasional "English" or "French" bed. There were beds much plainer than the carved ones we so much admire, but in any case the bed was the most valuable household possession, as it had always been. In 1640 William Southmead's house in Gloucester, Mass., is valued at £8, and his feather-bed, bedstead, and appurtenances at the same sum. In 1628 a pair of sheets was furnished to each Massachusetts Bay Colonist. Linen and flannel sheets were the ones in use. After spinning became universal and flax abundant, homespun sheets abounded,—"20 and 1 pr." is not an unusual number; and where there were several daughters whose chests had to be filled, the number was many times greater. Table linen also was of domestic manufacture.

One of the fashionable patterns of beds shown in the English books imported into the Colonies, and made by American cabinet-makers, was known as the "field bed." The one shown earlier in the chapter is in the Whipple House, Ipswich, and is draped with the netting curtains, heavily dotted and fringed, which were customary in its day. Early in 1700 there was an auction sale of Governor Cornbury's effects in New York, and the following advertisement concerning them:

"A fine yellow Camblet bed lined with silk and trimmed with fine lace, which came from London. One fine field bedstead and curtains. Some blue cloth lately come from London for liveries and some broad gold lace. A very fine medecine chest with a great variety of valuable medecines. A parcel of sweetmeats and jelly glasses. A case of 12 knives and 12 forks with silver handles. A large iron fireplace and iron bars all to be seen at the Fort.

It seemed as if the field bed had been made here, as it is specified that several of the other articles came from London. "The Journeyman's Cabinet &

Highboy

Chair-makers Philadelphia Book of Prices" gives in 1795 the price of a mahogany field bed, with sloped roof, at £1 7s., while one of poplar, with the roof sloped each way, cost but one pound. The carving of the posts was of course extra and was to be paid for according to time. Each inch that the bed was longer than six feet and wider than four feet was to be charged for at the rate of two pence per inch. This may be the reason why many of the beds were so narrow. It is often stated that the field bed was in use for a few years only, about the middle of the 18th Century, while in fact it was here, imported and of domestic make for fully one hundred years, and I am by no means sure that Governor Cornbury's was among the earliest.

Great attention was paid to the draping and arranging of the curtains, valances, and testers of the high four-posters. Heavy materials of silk and woollen were used, as well as cotton stuffs. Men paid great attention to the colourings of their bed furniture, as we have seen in several inventories, and Horace Walpole chose for his own bed at Strawberry Hill purple cloth lined with white satin, and bunches of feathers on the tester. Hepplewhite spent much pains on the details of his beds, and recommended that the valance be made very full, in which case it was called the "petticoat valance." There were also elaborate details for tying back the curtains and trimming them with gimp and fringe. The bed-drapings, even in early days, were often very valuable. Col. Francis Epes, of Henrico Co., Va., has in his inventory dated October 1, 1678:

Corner Cupboard

"One large new feather bed with camlett curtains and double vallins lind with yellow silke, bolster, pillow, counterpane, Rodds and hooks tops and stands, 1 curtaine and some Fringe damnified £24 5s. 0d."

The low-post bed was also a very handsome piece of furniture, and in many cases the post was surmounted by a pineapple, like the example shown earlier. This bed has passed through a career of violent contrasts, and it is only within a year that the four posts were rescued from a barn, where they afforded convenient roosts for poultry. The side and head and foot boards had passed entirely out of sight, no doubt in some moment of stress they had fed the family cooking-stove. The missing parts have been restored in solid mahogany, and it makes a very handsome piece of furniture. It belongs to Mr. William M. Hoyt, of Rochester, N. Y. The acanthus leaves on the lower parts of the legs are unusually handsome. The posts are 63 inches high, and the brass drops which conceal the screw-holes have been restored from a bed of the same period.

An unusually elegant example of the French bed is the one pictured. This bed is of rosewood, with legs of splendidly carved dolphins, and on the side rails and rolling ends are very rich ormolu decorations cut from solid brass. The medallions directly over the legs show Fame blowing her trumpet, and the rams' heads terminating the head and foot boards where they rest upon the wood above the stars are solid brass also. This bed has been many years in this country, and stood in the bridal chamber or guest-room of the old Van Rensselaer Manor House at Albany, N. Y. This room was situated on the ground floor to the right of the front door.

A most necessary piece of furniture which every housekeeper endeavoured to own was some form of "highboy," as it has come to be called, or a chest-on chest of drawers. On the previous page is a fair example of the highest style of perfection to which these articles reached. Few are found more ornate than this. The wood is mahogany, and is richly carved on the knees, with the upper and lower drawers ornamented with shell and scrolls. The escutcheons and handles are original, and the only defect is the loss of the two ornaments which decorated either side of the top. The date of this chest of drawers is anywhere from 1750 to about 1780, the overlapping drawers making it more likely to approximate the earlier date.

Belonging to about the same period is the corner cupboard shown in Figure 65. This is of cherry, with the broken arch-cornice and Gothic door. It has turned posts with rosettes which Sheraton often used, and the cupboard doors overlap and are panelled. The back of the cupboard is of pine, as are the shelves. The wood is a rich dark colour and unpolished. Similar pieces, though not exactly in this form, are to be met with in Virginia and are doubtless of native manufacture.

American makers used not only mahogany, cedar, ash, elm, pine, maple, cherry, poplar, and walnut, but could inlay with "King, tulip, rose, purple,

Inlaid and Lacquered Table and Chair

snake, zebra, Alexandria, panella, yew, and maple." There were cabinet-makers in every town, and many of them put out as handsome work as their contemporaries in London. In Chapter V mention has been made of the cabinet-makers of the eighteenth century, but furniture was made in the Colonies even before that. The native joiners began to work as early as 1622, for Phineas Pratt, of Weymouth, Mass., was what we now call a cabinet-maker, and before 1700 Boston had at least 25 cabinet-makers whose names appear in various records. We have also spoken of Connecticut chests, and their manufacture somewhere in that State. There is also another style known as the Hadley chest. Mr. Lockwood, in his fine work on furniture, places the date of these chests as ranging from 1690 to 1720. They come in one-, two-, and three-drawer patterns, varying in height from 32½ inches in one-drawer size to 46 inches for the three-drawer style. The peculiarity of these chests is their decoration, their shape being similar to other chests of the same period. In addition to being carved they are stained as well,—red, mulberry, and black being the colours chosen. On the central panel of the front the initials of the owner were usually roughly carved; the decoration of the chest, confined to the front, being a rude vine, while the sides are panelled. The top, body of drawers, and back of chest are always pine, the thrifty New England craftsman saving his hardwood for places where it would show. There is a very fine specimen of these Hadley chests in the Museum at Deerfield, Mass. Several more are in collections gathered in Massachusetts or adjoining States. The black-stained pine ornaments do not always mark a piece as of domestic manufacture, for pear-wood was used by the Dutch, and even occasionally by the English, stained black to imitate ebony, which was always more or less costly.

Lacquered Table

After 1725 there was considerable travel by merchants, and to a small extent by others bent on pleasure. Inns became of importance, and brought in good incomes to their owners. Abel Chapin kept a tavern at Chicopee, Mass., in 1730, and some few leaves of his account-book still remain. The records of the bar are the most numerous entries, and he sold there "Rhum & Cyder", bowls of punch and mugs of flip, and sometimes "Shugar, seed-corne, salt, and molasses." When this prosperous innkeeper died he left personal property valued at £400, and his real estate was worth £1,300. There were six hundred items mentioned in his inventory among the household furnishings, including iron, pewter, and brass ware with some china and glass. There is also special mention of "36 linen sheets, sixteen blankets, eleven woolen sheets, 6 table cloths and 21 towels." The inventory of his wardrobe shows richness for those days, and justifies his mother's statement that she had one son who was too rich. The inventory begins with:

"2 Great Cotes, 1 srait Body Cote, 1 pare lether Britches, 1 pare shues, 4 pare pumps, 1 hat, a black Velvet Vest, 1 pare Velvet Britches, 9 pare hose, 4 fine shirts, 6 common shirts, shoe Buckles."

His brother, a bachelor, died in 1747, and also had much worldly geer. He had "cotes and jackets of Camlet, serge and Broadcloth", and "some shirts, some more shirts, and some fine shirts."

There was no longer such great stress for the necessaries of life, in the Connecticut Valley at least, though there was still hardship and danger a plenty. Game and wild fowl abounded in the woods, and the rivers were full of fish. There is on record a single catch in one night of 6,000 shad and 90 salmon, six men being at work. Each householder was required to keep at least three sheep, and these, with the fields of flax, supplied bedding and clothing.

The Wayside Inn, South Sudbury, Mass., is still standing to show what a handsome and hospitable dwelling one of these old-fashioned inns was. Earlier we showed the old dining-room, looking today pretty much as it did over two centuries ago. On the left is a handsome lowboy with carving, and from the little alcove on the right many a steaming glass of flip or negus was served to cold and weary travellers. The dining-room was the centre of hospitality in the later Colonial days, as the kitchen had been in the earlier period. There was no handsomer or more hospitable entertainer than John Hancock, of Boston. In September, 1778,

Mahogany Bureau

he gave a dinner to Count D'Estaing, the French Admiral, and his officers and other dignitaries. There was such a large company that the spacious ball-room at the Hancock House was not large enough, so Faneuil Hall was engaged for the occasion. All contemporary accounts agree that it was a very splendid affair and went off with great *éclat*. The following amusing glimpse behind the scenes shows Mr. Hancock's anxiety about the provisions for this same dinner.

"MONDAY NOON, 30 Aug. 1778.

DEAR SIR—The Phillistines are coming upon me on Wednesday next at Dinner. To be Serious, the Ambassador, etc., etc., are to dine with me on Wednesday, and I have nothing to give them, nor from the present prospect of our Market do I see that I shall be able to get anything in Town. I must beg the fav^r of you to Recommend to my man Harry where he can get some chickens, Ducks, Geese, Hams, Partridges, Mutton or anything that will save my reputation in a dinner, and by all means some Butter. Be so good as to help me and you will much oblige me. Is there any good Mellons or Peaches or any good fruit near you? Your advice to Harry will much oblige me. Excuse me, I am very troublesome. Can I get a good Turkey? I walked in Town to-day. I dine on board the French Frigate to-morrow, so you see how I have Recovered. God bless you. If you see anything good at Providence, do Buy it for me.

JOHN HANCOCK."

Apparently the friend came to his assistance. The appearance of the company must have been very gay, for bright apparel was not confined to ladies alone.

Seven years later James Bowdoin, the Governor of Massachusetts (1785) on a review day at Cambridge, wore a grey wig, cocked hat, white broadcloth coat and vest, red small-clothes, and black-silk stockings. Thomas Jefferson wore a white coat and red breeches. The ladies were looked out for also, and—

"a neat assortment of women's and children's stays, also hoops and quilted coats, also men's and women's shoes from England"

were advertised in the "New York Mercury." As early as 1761 Mr. H. Levy offered for sale Hyson tea, coffee and chocolate, and English-made shoes.

The "New York Gazette" of May 15, 1789, describes a gown of the prevailing mode as follows:

"A plain but celestial blue satin gown over a white satin

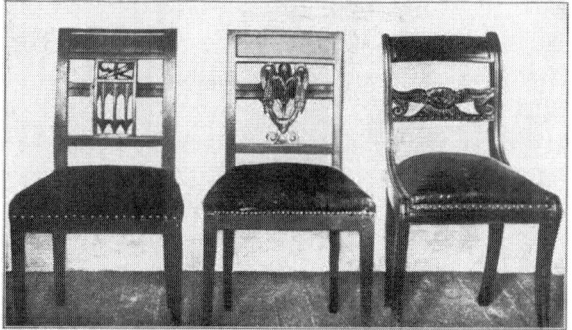

American Made Chairs

petticoat. Over the neck was worn a large Italian gauze handkerchief. Head-dress a pouf of gauze in form of a globe, the head-piece of which was made of white satin having a double wing which was trimmed with a wreath of roses. The hair was dressed in detached curls and a floating chignon."

At this same period in winter weather the gentlemen wore muffs of bearskin with knots of scarlet ribbon, while the hats of the ladies were so immense that it was suggested that a larger style of umbrella be invented so as to protect them.

From 1750 the decoration of the fireplace became of importance, and marble chimney-fronts, blue and white tiles, and beautifully variegated marble hearths in different colours are freely advertised. Carved and open-work mahogany mantelpieces could be had by 1765, and elegant grates and Bath Stoves are imported from England. Fire-dogs or andirons of many patterns are advertised for sale.

We have seen in many inventories how the elegances of the East crept in among stouter and more practical goods. The lacquered tables and chairs shown are two fine examples of Oriental lacquer-work ornamented with gold and inlaid with mother-of-pearl flowers. The chair is lacquered on some exceedingly light and porous wood, and has a cane seat. The table, which is of a very ornate design, has a heavy base to prevent its tipping over. Both belong to the Erastus Corning Estate, and are now at the Albany Historical Society Rooms. Music-stands were also made of lacquered wood and decorated with gilt patterns and mother-of-pearl.

Another very beautiful example of lacquer-work is shown earlier this chapter with the table. This is gold lacquer on black and special attention should be given to the Oriental rendering of the pillar and claw feet of the table. The carving is very fine, the dragon's head in which each foot terminates being quite a work of art. The vase which stands on the table is Sèvres, made under Napoleon's direction as a gift to the Emperor of Russia. It never reached its destination; for Napoleon himself went to Russia, and his mission was not to give, but to take. The vase was secured in Paris by Mr. William Bayard, and presented by him to his brother-in-law, General Stephen Van Rensselaer, the eighth patroon of Rensselaerwick.

American Made Rosewood Card Table

Bureaus with flat tops, upon which stood either lacquered or wooden dressing-glasses, were in use during the latter part of the eighteenth and in the early part of the nineteenth centuries. Sometimes the glasses were attached to the bureau itself, which then had an extra set of small drawers above the larger ones, set back so as to leave a shelf in front of them. Such a piece of a very ornate character is shown in Figure 68. It is of mahogany with gilt mountings of very beautiful design on the pillars of the front. The drawer which swells out has on it a splendid Empire gilt ornament. Above this the rail across the front is painted black and has a pattern in gold upon it. The curved supports to the mirror are carved and then painted with gold, as is the mirror-frame itself. The handles are glass, with bosses of gilt, completing an unusually handsome piece of furniture. The glass handles place the date of this bureau as not earlier than 1820.

The work of domestic furniture-makers has often been referred to in this work, and are given examples of three chairs, all of them mahogany, the two on the left being in Sheraton style, and the one on the right rather later, and coming under the head of Empire. The latter has the curved back and legs which were very popular, and a very distinctively American touch in the finely carved eagle which ornaments the cross-bar of the back.

All three chairs are well carved, and the panelled back of the middle one has a thread of brass moulding. The carved design is adapted from some well-known patterns by Sheraton. The one on the extreme left has some very delicate carving above the three arrows. In the little open panel are a bow and quiver quite out of proportion, in their size, to the large, heavy arrows below it. All three chairs had the covering nailed down with brass nails in the popular style, and the middle one

104

still has the original stuff. American cabinet-makers also excelled in making and carving very beautiful rosewood furniture which was held in high estimation down to the middle of the century. A piece of such work is shown in the handsomely carved card-table represented on the previous page.

The legs are gracefully curved and embellished with fine carving. The top turns, and then opens, a circular portion of the center being covered with cloth. Within the frame the table is finished with handsome curled maple, and has numerous little compartments for holding cards and counters. This specimen belongs to Miss Sarah Frost, of Rochester, N. Y.

French Furniture

THE glory of the French Renaissance had begun to wane when Louis XIII. came to the throne in 1614, and by the time of his death in 1643 it had become hardly more than a tradition.

Its strongest period had been during that century which embraced the reigns of five sovereigns, Francis I., and II., and Henry II., III., and IV. This was from 1515 to 1610, and, of all monarchs who held the throne of France, Francis I., who sat upon it thirty-two years, did more for it in raising the standard of art than had been done by his predecessors in a century, though Henry II. and Henry IV. had made their reigns notable.

French late Renaissance era walnut table - Image: David Jackson

Rich, ambitious to have France as great in art as Italy, Francis was a liberal patron, and invited to Paris, the centre of all literature and art in France, painters, sculptors, and architects. Italy had difficulties to contend with from the fact that she was divided into many small principalities and dominated by many schools. Florence, Milan, Sienna, Naples,—each had their distinctive styles; but in France the court of Francis was the pivot upon which all the arts turned. He built that series of chateaus which remain among the wonders of the world,—Chambord, Chenonceau, and Fontainebleau. He left traces of his

Image: Vivienne Gucwa

taste on mediæval Amboise, remodelled the Louvre, and finished the restoration of Blois which had been begun by Louis XII. The throes through which France has passed has swept away some of her choicest historic monuments, but Fontainebleau remains a true example of French Renaissance. With this fine old palace are connected some of the most critical moments of French history. In one of its rooms was signed the revocation of the Edict of Nantes; Condé was murdered here in the library, or Gallery of Diana. On the great curved staircase Napoleon bade adieu to what remained of the Old Guard before he went to Elba, and on a little table in one of the six rooms which might be called the suite of the First Empire, extending back of the gallery of Francis I. he signed his act of abdication.

The decorations of this palace are superb, the very flower of the French Renaissance. Oak, carved and gilded, wainscots the walls in many of the rooms, but in the chamber of Anne of Austria, shown in Figure 71, the wainscoting consists of carved panels framed in marbles, and above them carved figures stand out from the painted walls, which are divided by oak mouldings into sections, while a beautiful carved cornice of scallop-shells on a gold ground surrounds the room.

The French, as no other nation has ever done, set in a fitting shrine the beautiful furniture which they made; the decoration of walls, doors, ceilings, and fireplace always playing an important part in the whole scheme. The French "style," a word on which Lady Dilke strongly insists in her great work on "French Furniture of the XVIII Century," was unmistakably impressed on all they attempted. The woodwork was lighter and more openly carved than Italian work of the same period. Even when made by Italian workmen who swarmed to the French court under promise of abundant employment and rich emolument, the work was imbued with the French spirit and an elegance with which even Italy could not vie.

The noble appreciation which had grown up in France was fostered by Louis XIV. when he came to the throne, not so much for art's sake as for his own aggrandizement, and to make his court the most elegant in the world. Louis contemned the style of elegance and luxury begun in an earlier reign, and artists of even superior merit were set to work to make beautiful the homes of those uncrowned queens on whom the "Grand Monarch" lavished such immense sums of money. Versailles was enriched, the lovely gardens planned by Le Notre, with their superb flower beds and fountains, the "green carpet" of turf down which the monarch loved to walk, were all made with enormous outlay of money.

The hotels and buildings at Versailles set apart for the service of the king and his attendants were numbered by hundreds. There were the royal stables, the new hotel of the Governor of Versailles, the green rooms of the actors who performed at the palace, the hotel of the keeper of the wardrobe, the hotel of the guardsmen, the English garden, the riding-school, the king's icehouses, the houses of the body-guard, and so on. Street after street was filled with these buildings, besides those devoted to falconry, boar-hunting, the kennels, the little stables, and those filled with shops, vegetable gardens, etc., and in addition that great habitation occupied by more than two thousand persons, with other buildings called "Louises" where the king assigned temporary or permanent lodgings. The great stables built in 1682 and costing 3,000,000 francs are some of the few buildings left to show the magnificence of old Versailles. They were so ample and beautiful that under the direction of the great Louis himself they served sometimes as a ball-room, sometimes as a theatre, and more often as a circus for the princes.

There is a bound volume extant, bearing the name of Mansart, in which the cost of the palace is given at 153,000,000 francs. This was but the casket itself without any of its furnishings. Louis preferred to live in the open air, and the gardens were merely outdoor drawing-rooms, where people conversed and exchanged the compliments of the day. Round his person the king loved to group his retinue, and down the broad staircases of the gardens sixty ladies with hoopskirts measuring twenty-four feet in circumference could move easily. On the outskirts were a swarm of courtiers and servants in uniforms, costumes, and liveries as brilliant as the rainbow.

Consider the life of one of these courtiers under the reign of Louis XIV. Here is the routine of the Duc de La Rochefoucauld, Master of the Hounds:

—"He never missed the king's rising or retiring, both changes of dress every day, the hunts and promenades likewise every day, for ten years in succession. Never sleeping away from the place where the king rested, not able to stay away all night, and yet obliged to dine away from court."

Even after the court etiquette became more stiff and precise, and the formal manners arranged by Louis and Madame de Maintenon were in daily practice, the smaller details of life remained as elegant as possible. Hoopskirts of such size as has been mentioned were too enormous for chairs, so a sort of stool without arms or back became a necessary article of furniture. One sofa, two arm-chairs, and nine stools were a proper proportion for a set to furnish a room, and these were stiffly set about the walls, leaving the middle of the room quite bare.

We also show part of the bedroom of Louis XIV. at Versailles, with the elaborate decorations which were lavished on that palace, and the furniture which accompanied it. Tapestry-covered chairs and hangings of the richest embroidery were all in harmony with the splendid walls. The tall bronze girandoles were Cupids supporting branches of flowers in ormolu to hold candles. Over the doors were portraits or mirrors surmounted by carved and gilt figures with garlands of flowers. The decorated Boulle cabinet on the right is very different in its lines from those articles as seen in the succeeding reign, when everything assumed a lighter air. The curtains to the bed could completely enfold it, and to their sheltering depths the great Louis is said to have retired before removing his wig.

The chairs shown on the following page are of this period, the one upon the right retaining its original covering, the woodwork being carved and gilt. The cane chair on the left is of walnut, and the one in the centre, carved and gilt, is a French adaptation of a Flemish design.

It is difficult to re-people one of these splendid rooms and consider a period when, as M. Taine says, "life was wholly operatic." The grandee lived in a state of luxury and grandeur. His trappings were as magnificent as he could make them, and his household was filled with military as well as civil appointments, approaching as nearly to that of the king as possible.

The king must have a stable, so at Versailles were 1,875 horses, 217 vehicles, and 1,458 men who were clothed in liveries costing 540,000 francs a year. This is but a single item in the great total considered under fifty or sixty heads. To wait on the king himself, 198 persons were required; some fetched his mall and balls; some combed his hair; others watched his dogs; and there were those who tied his necktie after it had been properly folded. Some there were whose sole business it was to stand in a corner which was not to be left empty.

The policy which prescribed the custom at court was all for ostentatious display. St. Simon says:

Chairs of the Period of Louis XIV

"He (Louis XIV.) was pleased to see a display of dress, table, equipages, buildings, and play; these afforded him opportunities for entering into conversation with people. The contagion had spread from the court into the provinces and to the armies, where people of any position were esteemed only according to their table and magnificence."

Louis had so dominated the whole court life that he had brought his courtiers to believe that the main thing in life for layman and churchman, and for women and men alike, was to be at all hours and in every place under the king's eye and within reach of his voice.

With all this army of personal attendants to feed, clothe, and shelter, the repairs to houses and furniture represented immense sums yearly, and many establishments were taken under royal patronage in order to command their products and to reduce the expenditures.

The history of French furniture is quite closely connected with the history of tapestry, for after a time it was used as a covering. Francis I., who appreciated the value of this textile as an ornament as well as a covering for his walls, and unwilling to buy all his pieces from the skilful looms of Flanders, started a factory in 1531 at Fontainebleau. In 1603 a new factory was started at Paris, under royal patronage, in the workshop of a family of dyers named Gobelin. The first workers were Flemish weavers who were brought over to teach the craft to Frenchmen. Louis XIV. protected the factory through the mediumship of that great financier, Colbert, who appointed Le Brun, the artist, director of the works. In 1667 the factory became the property of the Crown, and most artistic and elegant productions were made.

Not only in France did the Gobelins find patronage, but in England as well their work was in great demand. Evelyn writes in the last years of the reign of Charles II.:

—"Here I saw the new fabriq of French tapisstry; for designe, tendernesse of worke, and incomparable imitationn of the best paintings beyond anything I ever beheld. Some pieces had Versailles, St. Germain's, and other palaces of the French King, with huntings, figures, and landskips, exotiq fowls, and all to the life rarely don."

The golden age of Louis XIV. saw also the golden age of tapestry, for it was during his reign that the proud and royal factory at Aubusson was at its highest estate. The tapestries sent out from this factory were not mere imitations as

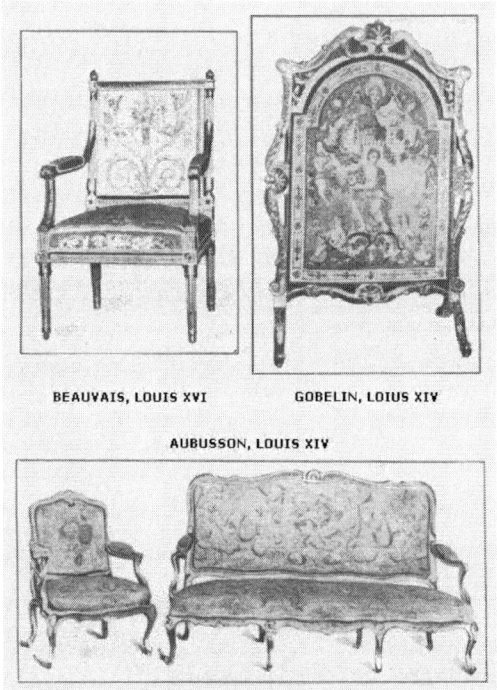

BEAUVAIS, LOUIS XVI   GOBELIN, LOIUS XIV

AUBUSSON, LOUIS XIV

Tapestry Furniture

close as possible of painted pictures. The limitations of the process were ever considered, and the number of gradations in every tint was limited so that the dangers of unequal fading reached their lowest point. The beautiful borders which surrounded the central picture were designed and executed with the same care that was bestowed on the centre, and formed a part of the whole that could ill be spared.

The tapestries worked late in the seventeenth century and early in the eighteenth, before the spirit of commercialism had been suffered to encroach on what up to that time had been carefully fostered art work, were all examples of great beauty and merit. In 1694, Louis having lost interest in the manufactory, and Colbert and Le Brun being dead, the works at the Gobelins' factories declined, and they became financially embarrassed. Still the great name was in high esteem, and its more than national reputation was retained.

110

The splendid works which had been sent out from the loom, "The Triumph of Alexander," "The History of the King," "The Elements," and "The Seasons," were no longer in demand. Fontaine's fables and "The Adventures of Don Quixote" took the place of the more dignified designs, and at last sets of chair-backs and sofa covers were woven where previously historic subjects of heroic size had been demanded. Every year there were "*Chancelleries*" made,—series of hangings adorned with the royal arms, which the king gave to his chancellors.

"The Adventures of Don Quixote" consisted of a set of from twenty to twenty-eight pieces, and so pleased the public taste that sets were being continually woven from 1723 till the times of the Revolution. They were varied by the different colours of the background, and also by having different borders, some of them designed by artists like Lemaire the younger, and of great beauty. By 1736 the manufactory once more received assistance and patronage from the Crown, and famous old models were renewed, and two new sets, from "The Story of Esther," and "The Story of Medea and Jason," were designed.

About the middle of the century came the fatal desire to copy paintings as they came from the hand of the artist, and the traditions which had governed the labor of the tapestry-worker for centuries were thrown aside. In vain the workmen protested: good taste and the principles of decoration were sacrificed, and the artist triumphed. The only check to the artist's exactions was the immense cost of production, for the

Commodes of the Time of Louis XV

painter was totally ignorant of the practical difficulties which had to be overcome in carrying out his designs; and as the tapestry-workers were paid by the piece they could no longer calculate or limit the cost of execution.

The Beauvais tapestries were long granted superior excellence in flower forms, trees, etc., and for figures also, and they held to the styles in which they excelled. But the Gobelins after 1740 no longer did work which was not fashionable and profitable. In 1755 Boucher, the well-known artist, was appointed director of the Gobelins, and, like his predecessors, believed in simulating, as far as possible the painter's art. There is tragedy in the history of the devoted band of workers who, ill-paid, and not sufficiently recognized, laboured at the looms and in the dye-house to carry out the artist's ideas. One of them Quimiset, a chemist of undoubted ability, committed suicide. Neilson and Audran were both ruined financially; and

111

yet these servants of the crown were not allowed to leave Paris to better their fortunes.

The Gobelins began to produce tapestry for furniture only during the last half of the eighteenth century. This work was undertaken in hopes of financial profit, for the competition of woven and embroidered stuffs from England, as well as the novelty of English paper-hangings, had crippled them excessively. The very first pieces made were for four chairs and a sofa, in 1748. These furniture tapestries became immediately popular. Screens, seat, sofa and chair backs, showing scenes, figures, ribbon-work, and garlands brought up the failing fortune of Gobelin and made Beauvais wealthy. From this latter factory came those coverings, with designs after Boucher, set in wooden frames of the richest carving and gilt.

The cost of these works was as great as brocade and velvet, and crowded out the embroiderers, who in turn aimed, with the means at their command, to rival the efforts of the tapestry-workers. Then came that most sumptuous combination of painting with embroidery, and in 1743 the Duc de Luynes describes a new set of furniture for the queen's bedroom.

"It is of white gros de Tours, embroidered and painted, and is quite complete, consisting of the bed, its hangings, the fauteuils, and curtains."

During the Revolution, in 1793, a bonfire was made in the courtyard of the Gobelin factory, and a set of hangings with designs of "The Visit of Louis XIV. to the Gobelins," several *portieres*, and a set of "*Chancelleries*" were burned. On another visit the cartoons of Raphael were destroyed, those of "Esther" and "Medea" thrown out, and everything with a tendency toward aristocracy discarded.

The terms "Beauvais," "Aubusson," etc., do not give their names to any particular style of tapestry. The various factories wove according to their requirements, and used silk, woolen, silver and gold thread as the design called for it. In the image of the tapestry furniture are examples of work from these famous establishments. The Louis XIV. screen is a silk panel, the pattern being Flora, surrounded by Cupids and wreaths and garlands of flowers. The design is by Berain, and was made at the Gobelins; the frame is richly carved and gilt.

The Louis XVI. chair is covered with Beauvais tapestry—baskets of flowers and scrolls. The lovely tints are hardly faded, or they have so faded in harmony that it resembles the changing hues of mother-of-pearl. The wooden frame is carved and gilded, a fit setting for the beautiful tapestry. The sofa and chair are but two of a set, the other pieces being nine more chairs. These are of the Louis XIV. period and are covered with Aubusson tapestry,—crimson peonies on a pale-green ground. The bow leg and carved knees are similar to those shown earlier, and, like the one on the right in that illustration are gilded.

At a recent sale held in Paris, when the great collection of Madame Lelong was dispersed, the prices obtained for these old tapestries, whether wall-coverings or on furniture, were absolutely astonishing. A screen with four panels of Beauvais tapestry illustrating La Fontaine's fables brought $3,700. One seat, of carved and gilded wood, covered with a piece of Beauvais, brought $2,000, and four chairs in carved and gilded wood with Beauvais tapestry coverings brought $41,000. These prices, while sensational, give some idea of the esteem in which these antiques are held. The tapestry covered pieces shown belong to the Waring Galleries, London.

The best-known name of any one man who worked in furniture during the splendid reign of Louis XIV. was of André-Charles Boulle, b. 1642, d. 1732. The superb marquetry work he made, composed of brass, ivory, tortoise-shell, gold, and a choice selection of woods from India, Brazil, and other tropical countries, took the fancy of the king by reason of its sumptuous nature. Boulle was given an apartment in the Louvre and for his great master the celebrated *ébéniste* composed his choicest work. A cabinet of this work can be seen to the right of the bed pictured earlier.

In 1672 Louis XIV. had made Boulle engraver-in-ordinary of the royal seals. The patent conferring this appointment calls Boulle "architect, painter, carver in mosaic, artist in cabinet work, chaser, inlayer, and designer of figures." The most important works of Boulle which records show were at Versailles, like those he executed for foreign princes, have disappeared. His workshops and studios were of vast extent; he employed many workmen, and consulted for his models a priceless collections of drawings, medals, and gems, comprising drawings by Raphael, and that "manuscript journal kept by Rubens during his travels in Italy and elsewhere, which contained his notes and studies in painting and sculpture, copiously illustrated by pen-and-ink sketches."

In "French Furniture of the XVIII Century," by Lady Dilke, this priceless collection belonging to Boulle is described at length, and also the immense loss to which this worker was subjected when, in 1720, his entire warehouses and shops were burned down. Boulle was an old man at this time, and for the rest of his life ill-fortune followed him, and he died wretchedly poor, leaving nothing but debts which for years he had been forced to put off by every variety of makeshift. His four sons, one of whom bore his father's name, never accomplished works of such elegance and solidity as those of their father. They, too, had endless misfortune, were ejected from the apartment in the Louvre which had descended to them from their father, and died, as he did, in poverty and misery.

Garderobe, Period of Louis XV.

Yet the splendid and showy style of furniture to which Boulle gave his name remained in fashion and was made during the whole of the eighteenth century. After the death of the younger Boulles, pupils who had studied with their father and themselves carried on the work, and of course there were imitators as well. Boulle did not invent this style of decoration, for ebony cabinets ornamented with tortoise-shell and copper were known in France long before Boulle was born. He simply perfected the method of making it. Nor did he confine himself to this particular style of marquetry, for he made works, mentioned in his catalogue, of wood inlaid with other woods of various colours and ornamented with bronze mounts.

Bedroom of Marie Antionette at the Little Trianon

Under the Regency, fashions changed, not only in manners and clothes, but even in furniture and belongings as well, though this latter change came slowly. The Duc d'Orleans and his daughter, the Duchesse de Berri, conducted entertainments of so scandalous a nature that even the French public was horrified; and gaming, which under Louis XIV. had risen to prodigious extremes, became more furious still, and, possessing all classes of society, spread ruin everywhere. The use of looking-glasses for ornaments had become very much the vogue during the period of Louis XIV.'s reign. They were introduced into walls opposite windows, and in places where reflection would carry out the idea of windows. The court beauties, both male and female, had the walls of their bathrooms lined with them, and the frames in which they were set were lavishly carved and gilded.

While Boulle's is associated with the reign of Louis XIV., with the Regency the name of Charles Cressent rose to eminence. His work was much like that of Boulle in character, but he gradually gave more importance to the mounts of metal as a means of ornament, and used less marquetry. He not only used floral forms for these metal decorations, but modelled beautiful little groups of Cupids or Loves with garlands and roses, and these ornaments were applied directly to the rosewood frames of wardrobe or cabinet, whichever was chosen for such embellishment. Nor was he content with such charming subjects only, for he modelled children swinging a monkey, or monkeys swinging themselves, or dancing a tight rope, and invested even these grotesques with style and charm.

With the reign of Louis XV. even more sumptuous surroundings were desired. At Fontainebleau the luxury was unparalleled, and when the king held a reception, at which there were both cards and dancing, the spectacle, according to records left in the copious memoirs of the times, was one of sumptuous elegance. Four or five hundred guests surrounded the tables where cards and cavagnole were played. Hanging from the ceiling painted with Cupids garlanded with flowers, were many blazing chandeliers, their brilliancy reflected a thousand times in the tall mirrors. Everything was flooded with light,—the painted walls, the rich gilding, the diamonds sparkling on white necks and in the hair of the women, whose dresses gleamed with gold, silver, pearls, and artificial flowers and fruits, all in the most gorgeous hues. The men were almost as gay. Their hair was powdered, curled, and dressed. Their coats of sky-blue, rose, peach, pearl or puce-colored satin, velvet, or brocade, were embroidered with silks and gold, and ornamented with ruffles and cravats of lace. The dress of a man, with his jewelled sword, shoulder-knots with diamond tags, and buckles of brilliants on shoe and knee, might have cost a small fortune. Gold and silver thread made stiff and costly, stuffs already rich in themselves, while the money lavished on lace had no limit.

When a princess of France married it was no uncommon thing for the laces on her

Chairs and Table of Louis XVI Style

bedspreads and linens to reach the sum of $100,000. The frills on her personal linen added $25,000 more. The ruffle on a handkerchief was cheap at $50, and a laced nightcap might easily double that. All this elaboration of elegance had fitting surroundings, and the case was worthy of its contents.

Like his predecessor, Louis XV. lavished vast sums on buildings, and Madame de Pompadour, an uncrowned queen, spent millions more. The Hotel d'Evreux, begun in 1718, was many years later finished under her personal direction. She had the virtue of being a liberal patron of the arts and an encourager of artistic merit wherever she found it. Her taste, her sincere love for art, enabled her at least to secure works of absolute perfection, and during the twenty years of her reign it was mainly her fostering guidance which developed so many of the applied arts. She not only assumed the direction of work at her chateaus and hotels, but she encouraged the manufactory of the beautiful porcelain of Sèvres; she assisted engravers, and essayed to learn the art herself; and by taste, natural and acquired, she was looked upon by the group of artists of her time as a final court of appeal in all critical matters.

Her successors were no less extravagant, but they lacked her exquisite and artistic judgment, which amounted almost to genius. It was during this period of Louis XV. that the evolution of chests of drawers, writing-tables, and cabinets— that is chests upon trestle-work—was accomplished. The ornament changed constantly, but the form of the articles remained much the same. The changes wrought in Paris affected the country slowly, and provincial artists working at the period of Louis XV. might have been using the models that had been popular in a previous reign. In the image of the depicted rosewood commodes with curved fronts and ends, handsomely decorated with ormulu work in leaves and scrolls. A French clock of the period, with ormulu mounts, stands on the marble top of one, and on the other is one of black and gold lacquer, with very choice water-gilt mounts.

Encoignure, Period of Louis XVI.

In this period the names of the Caffieri, father and two sons, who were workers in metal, became famous. They executed bronze mounts for furniture like those on the commodes shown earlier, a style which they may be said to have created and by their genius rendered popular. The mounting on these pieces is very simple, and takes the subservient place that ornament always should. But in some of the work executed by the Caffieri the wood became merely the vehicle on which a wealth of ornament was hung. They made not only mounts for furniture, but girandoles, branch-lights, mounts for vases and clocks, and chandeliers— working in bronze and silver as well as in brass. This taste for metal mounts was carried to an extreme, even pieces of richly carved furniture being further ornamented with chiselled brass. It is an item of interest that the monument to General Montgomery which is placed on that side of St. Paul's Chapel, New York city, which faces Broadway, should have been designed and executed by Caffier in Paris in 1777. The General was buried first in Quebec, and afterward removed to New York by act of Congress.

The image afterwards depicts what is called a *garderobe*: that is wardrobe, with a basket of flowers at the top, this and the two bunches of flowers at the tops of the doors being in ormolu.

Even as early as the middle of the previous century there had been imitators of the splendid lacquer-work of the Orient. By 1723 the three Martin Brothers, Julien, Robert, and Simon-Etienne, had become quite famous for their use of a transparent varnish, which, as "master painters and varnishers," they had perfected in their business. They pushed their trade, and by 1748 were under national protection, so

116

popular had their wares become. In 1742 they perfected a certain green varnish which was immensely popular, and for which they had many orders, some of them from the king himself.

They never excelled as painters, but the beauty of this famous green ground, powdered with gold, is very charming. Very little of this famous work remains, a few fire-screens and some splendid coaches, with some small boxes for snuff or patches, are all that exist. But in these small pieces like the boxes, which were considered worthy of gold and jewelled mounts, we can see this famous work to the best advantage. There were ribbings, stripings, waves, and flecks which gleam wonderfully through the varnish. Sometimes there are a few flowers or a Cupid scattered on the surface, but usually, when the green ground was employed, no decoration was considered necessary. With the death of Robert Martin in 1765 the skill necessary to continue this work was lost, and this charming style of decoration dropped back merely to a trade, and "Vernis-Martin" became hardly more than a name.

Among the other great workers of this period were Oeben, whose marquetry in coloured woods was of extreme elegance,

Bed of Josephine at Fontainebleau

and Riesener, who began to execute his beautiful pieces of furniture under Louis XV. in what is known as his earlier style, but who finally created the straight-legged types of Louis XVI. style with which his name became associated. In the work which he did for Marie Antoinette at the Little Trianon in 1777, the pure Louis XVI. style is carried out. The earlier pieces, delivered as early as 1771, still betray the influence of a previous period.

A few pages ago we showed the bedroom of Marie Antoinette at the Little Trianon. Here we see the later style set by Riesener, with the straight carved legs, the woodwork being painted and gilded. The silk factories at Lyons were no longer as well patronized as they had been, and to revive interest in them new furniture was ordered for the queen, to be upholstered in brocade, and with curtains and hangings to match. Everything in these rooms breathes of dainty elegance,—the carvings of the mantelpiece, the walls decorated with garlands of flowers and Cupids, even the metal mounts, chiselled wreaths and rosettes, were wrought with the beauty and finish of goldsmith's work. In the small chair by the bedside is seen

117

a style with gilt framework and embroidered cushions, a kind of covering which was always in demand.

In 1770 two coaches were sent to Vienna for Marie Antoinette. The work of the embroiderer was selected to embellish their interiors, and the description of them is given by Bachaumont:

"They were two berlins, much larger than usual, but yet not so large as those of the king. One is lined with rose velvet and the Four Seasons are embroidered on the largest cushions, with all the attributes of a festival. The other is lined with blue velvet, and on the cushions of this are worked the Four Elements. There is not a touch of painting about them, but the work of the artist is so perfect and finished that each one is a complete work of art."

The name of the embroider was Treaumau, and so celebrated did the beauty of these royal cushions make him that he received large orders, the most important being one from Madam de Berri for a *vis-à-vis*. The two berlins for Marie Antoinette were placed on exhibition before they were sent to her, and constituted an event of the day.

The three pieces shown earlier are pure types of Louis XVI. style. They are at the Cooper Institute, New York. The chair on the right has its original embroidered cover, and the straight carved leg so much in evidence. All three pieces are entirely gilt wherever the woodwork shows. The top of the table is marble. The chair to the left is very prettily carved with a torch and bow and arrows, according to the conceit of the times, when everything was to be joyous and gay, all suffering and sorrow being resolutely thrust out of sight. Rose, blue, and gold were the colours affected, nothing sombre being allowed. The whole life was careless and without responsibility. The letters of the day, Saint-Beuve, Comte de Tilly, Duc de Lauzun, and Madam d' Oberkirk, draw graphic pictures of the life of pleasure. The Duc de Lauzun says that one of his mother's lackeys, who could read and write tolerably well, was made his tutor.

"They gave me the most fashionable teachers besides, but M. Roche (the tutor) was not qualified to arrange their lessons, nor to qualify me to benefit by them. I was, moreover, like all the children of my age and station, dressed in the handsomest clothes to go out, and naked and dying with hunger in the house."

This was not through unkindness, but because of dissipation and carelessness, all the time and attention being given elsewhere. Even in the last days of the *ancien régime* little boys had their hair powdered and dressed in ringlets and curls. They wore a sword, carried a chapeau under the arm, wore laces and frills, and coats with cuffs heavy with gold lace. The small girls were their mothers in miniature. At six one of them would present her hand for a little dandy to kiss, her little figure would be squeezed into a stiff corset, her huge hoop-skirt supported a skirt of brocade enwreathed with garlands of flowers. On her head was a structure of false curls, puffs, knots, and ribbons, held on by pins and topped with plumes; and if she was pale they would put rouge on her face. By force of habit and instruction she bore herself like a mature woman. Her most important instructor was the dancing-master, her never-ending study deportment.

In the eighteenth century drawing-room women were queens. They prescribed the law and fashion in all things. There was no situation, however delicate, that they did not save through tact and politeness. This was the time when first Watteau, and later Lancret and Fragonard, painted the *Fêtes galantes*, when pretty picnics and dancing in a woody dell were great diversions. It was an idealized life of the brilliant world of France which early in the eighteenth century Watteau painted. Scattered all through the land were sumptuous dwellings of the rich, upon which fortunes were lavished. Beaus and belles alike dressed themselves *à la Watteau*. He became the lover's poet, a painter of an ideal pastoral which hardly existed, but to which his hand gave beauty and value. This was one side. On the other, besides heavy taxation, poor crops, flood, famine, and the devastation of war, there was always the pest. This terrible contagious fever, with the smallpox, was a scourge to the people. Hundreds fell victims to these twin plagues, for the usual treatment was copious bleeding.

But the court, while it might suffer at times from sickness and death, never allowed itself

Bed of Napoleon at Grand Trianon

to think of such things. It amused itself with balls and masques, plays, and even with blindman's-buff. The gardens at Versailles were always in gala dress, and at night musicians played among the trees, and thousands of lights sparkled among the flowers. Fifty years later they played at simplicity too, these great ladies and elegant cavaliers, laying aside the silks and brocades of which a surfeit had wearied them, and wearing picturesque gowns of simple material and cut. Marie Antoinette herself set the example in her retreat at Little Trianon, with the muslin gown and fichu crowned with a straw hat, in which she ran across the gardens. Beneath all this elegance, amiability, and extravagance the Revolution seethed and boiled and finally overran and destroyed. Till almost the very end extravagance increased, and earlier is shown an encoignure, or corner cupboard with commode below, and cabinet above, of the most elaborate inlaid work, with very rich ormolu mounts. This work is by David de Luneville, and is a marvel of the intricacy of inlaying, many different woods being used in that jumble of ornament which forms the decoration of the door in the cabinet. At each intersection of the lattice work inlay is a little rosette. The divisions of the lower part have an edging of satin-

119

wood, which in the centre panel is made more ornate with an inlay of ebony. This piece is at the Waring Galleries, London.

The new conditions in France wrought changes in every detail of life. Simplicity, so called, was becoming the watchword, and once more antique models were sought for forms and decorations. Under the Empire the style was much less graceful, the lines coarser, and the elaboration of ornament heavy. Could anything be less pleasing than Josephine's bed at Fontainebleau, shown in It is one of the few unsightly things in that beautiful palace, where are now gathered so many works of art. The bedstead is covered with heavy chiselled ornaments in brass, and surmounted by a canopy held on pillars. This canopy is partly of carved wood and partly of embroidered satin. There are strings of gold beads hanging from this satin, and in addition heavy satin curtains very richly embroidered. These are edged with a long and clumsy fringe. The whole room is in keeping with the bed, for the floor is covered with a carpet bearing the imperial insignia all over it, and the hangings on the walls have countless spots in lieu of a pattern. It was at Fontainebleau that the sentence of divorce was passed on Josephine, and it seems possible that the sleepless nights which the poor lady endured must have been rendered more miserable by the unlovely character of her surroundings.

It is with pleasure that one turns to the image on the previous page, showing the bed of the great Emperor himself, at Grand Trianon, Versailles. It is a good example of the best Empire work, and is mahogany ornamented with ormolu mounts in classic style.

It was now the fashion to decry the furniture or costumes which had prevailed during the latter half of the eighteenth century, and to seek the Athenian models for gowns and furniture. Nor were these models used in their simple shapes, but transformed into quite other guise by the touch of French hands. Marquetry was no longer considered good taste, and David the painter was largely responsible for much of the theatrical effect which was noted both in costume and household belongings. After the fall of the monarchy, sales had been held, and what had not been destroyed had been sold. It was now necessary to fill again the palaces that had been denuded, and Percier, the architect, and Joseph Desmalter, the cabinet-maker, were the men chosen to do it. Desmalter is responsible for the use of mahogany commodes embellished with bronze and gilt like those which flank the bed of Napoleon. After the expedition to Egypt, Sphynx figures were introduced in bronze or brass to uphold tables and as arms for chairs. These, however, did not become popular, and soon were replaced by classic heads.

In the picture on the previous page is shown a room in Fontainebleau furnished in Empire style. The imperial N may be seen on the corners of the console tables and on the commode. The walls are covered with damask woven in geometric forms, and the rooms once so light and brilliant with their dainty arabesques and flowers, Cupids and birds on the ceilings, are now dark and severe. The splendid chandelier of Venetian glass is the sole reminder of a previous reign. The only piece of furniture in the room which is absolutely plain is the small mahogany table in the foreground. Upon this Napoleon signed his abdication. In one of the rooms adjoining the leave-taking between Josephine and Napoleon occurred, after which he went to St. Cloud and she to Malmaison.

The commode shows as well as anything the marked change which took place in the styles under the Empire. The graceful curves of front and sides are gone; the feet are stumpy, and so short that the pleasing proportion between the parts is quite lost. The constant repetition of the laurel-wreath on chairs, walls, mantelpieces and furniture is very monotonous, and we miss the graceful curves of the acanthus and celery leaves.

In the image on the following page is a mahogany reading and writing desk combined. The brass ornaments are beautifully chiselled, and, though some are lost, enough remain to show what a splendid piece of furniture it once was. They partake, in their delicacy, of the metal work of the previous century, particularly the escutcheons and the groups of flowers and musical instruments which are on the tops of the side pillars. The desk top lifts up, and inside there are pigeon-holes and drawers finished in satin-wood. The hole in

Empire Reading and Writing Desk

the rail above the doors is not a keyhole, but in it fits a handle by which the whole upper part of the desk is raised on an iron rod so as to suit the height of who-ever uses it. This piece is at the Museum of the Cooper Institute. The rage for furniture in Empire style was not confined to France alone, but crossed the channel to England, where it became even less attractive, and was also used by our own cabinet-makers, as has been shown in previous chapters.

The changes in the styles of French furniture, like those which took place in England in the same century (the eighteenth), were not any more definitely marked. One period overlapped another, certain characteristics were retained and put to new uses, so that a perfect style was arrived at only after years of growth.

With the name of Louis XIV. is associated the furniture of Boulle, with its wealth of wonderful inlay. The metal mount in its most correct and elegant form marks the period of Louis XV. The reign of Louis XVI. and Marie Antoinette shows the change from the graceful curves of leg and construction lines to straight lines and less generous proportions, while the use of the metal mount is brought to the greatest extreme. The beauty of form taken from leaf and shell, wrought in metal and placed on the lines of fine construction which had marked the epoch of Louis XV., ran wild under the workers in the next era, and the fancy for overlaying with costly ornament blinded the eyes to the poor shapes employed, which were inspired by a search among classic forms. Even the severest form may become vulgar when overloaded with ornament, and with the reign of Louis XV. passed the production of some of the finest furniture ever made. What was poor under Louis XVI. became poorer yet under the Napoleonic era, and the men employed, instead of drawing from the choice models which still remained, still farther debased what in previous times had risen to the dignity of high art.

Musical Instruments

THE evolution of the piano from the clavichord occupied the attention of musicians for over three hundred years, or from 1404, when the earliest record occurs, to 1720, when Cristofori's piano was completed in Florence. The next instrument in the upward development after the clavichord was the virginal, a parallelogram in shape, with a projecting keyboard. Then came the spinet. The earliest of these now in existence is in Paris, and was made at Verona in 1523. By 1703 two Englishmen, Thomas and John Hitchcock, father and son, had made a great advance in the construction of spinets, giving them a wide compass of five octavos from G to G.

It was not until about 1660, after the restoration of the Stuarts, that the name "harpsichord" was given to the long wing-shaped instrument, similar to our grand piano, which had hitherto been called *clavecembalo* in Italy, *flügel* in Germany, and *clavecin* in France. Early in the sixteenth century the progressive Dutch had put into use double keyboards and stops. These were imported into England, and to John Haward is due the credit for the idea of pedals for the harpsichord. This was in 1676. This Haward was a fashionable instrument-maker in the days of the lively Pepys, who mentions him several times. Thus in April, 1668, he records:

—"Took Aldgate Street in my way, and then did call upon one Haward, who makes virginals, and there did like of a little espinette, and will have him finish it for me; for I had a mind to a small harpsicon, but this takes up less room."

The little espinette took some time to finish; for in July he says:

—"while I to buy my espinette, which I did now agree for, and did at Haward's meet with Mr. Thacker, and heard him play on the harpsicon so as I never heard man before, I think."

On the 15th of July the bargain is concluded; for he states, under that date:

"At noon is brought home the espinette I bought the other day of Haward; cost me £5."

A few days later he combines business with pleasure, for he notes:

"To buy a rest for my espinette at the ironmonger's by Holborn Conduit, where the fair pretty woman is, that I have lately observed there."

To follow is an image of a very beautiful spinet made by Domenico di Pesaro, in Italy, in 1661. The instrument can be taken from its outer case, is of cedar wood, has a projecting keyboard, and is decorated with ivory studs. The outer case is very handsome, decorated with *gesso* work, (which was so much copied by Robert Adam after his return from Italy) this work being gold on a pale-green ground. The decoration on the inside of the cover is a boating scene, the keys are of light wood, the sharps being black. The instrument, triangular in shape, rests on three richly carved and gilt legs, and is four feet eight inches long, by nineteen inches wide. It looks very tiny, even beside a "baby grand."

The beauty and enrichment of the cases in which these instruments were placed shows with what care and reverence they were regarded. Harpsichords varied much in having one, two, or occasionally three banks of keys, and being placed in upright cases, the covers of which opened like a bookcase, or in a horizontal case, as in the one shown later in this part. Each of the three banks of keys has a compass of five octaves, from F to F. The entire case is gilt Louis XV. style, decorated with elaborate carvings and with paintings of flowers and figures in medallions and borders. On the outside of the cover is the coat of arms of the Strozzi family. The name of the maker is engraved on an ivory plate above the keyboards, and reads—

VICENTIUS SODI FLORENTIUS FECIT.
ANNO DOMINI 1779.

The length of the case is seven feet; it is three feet wide, and nearly ten inches deep.

The harpsichord held its own for fifty years after the invention of the pianoforte, for Bartolommeo Cristofori published his invention as early as 1711, although he did not perfect his piano till 1720. His action has the escapement, without which there can be no vibrating note, and the "check," which was an all-important step toward repeating notes. There are preserved at Potsdam, Germany, three pianos which belonged to Frederick the Great, and which were made by

Organ in St. Michael's Church, Charleston, S. C.

Silberman, who exactly copied the action as well as the structure of Cristofori's invention. Later in this chapter is a picture of the first piano made by Cristofori. Above the front board is the following inscription:

BARTHOLOMÆUS DE CHRISTOPHORIS PATAVINUS INVENTOR
FACIERAT FLORENTIÆ MDCCXX

This instrument, as well as the two previously shown, belong to the collection of musical instruments given by Mrs. Crosby Brown to the Metropolitan Museum, New York.

This crude instrument bears testimony to years of patient endeavour. Like so many old and valuable treasures this one was harboured many years for sentimental reasons only, and because it had been given to an only daughter by her father. The story of the discovery of its value came about as follows, as told in a letter by Signor Martelli, to whose mother the piano belonged.

"For the sake of economy during the time that Florence was the capital of Italy, we rented the first floor of our house, No. 3, Via del Melarancio, and occupied the second floor. In 1872 Signora Martelli (my mother) again changed her apartments from the second to the first floor, and at the moment the transfer of our furniture was taking place from one floor to the other, Prof. Cosimo Conti, a scholar and intimate friend of ours, came to visit us. The professor, who was in close correspondence with Cavaliere L. Puliti, who was spending a great deal of his time in trying to discover the origin of the piano, discovered on it to his great surprise an inscription which attested that it had been made by Bartolomeo Christofori. He immediately informed Cavaliere L. Puliti of this fact, and he came at once to examine it. Then it was ascertained that it was one of the rarest and most valuable pianos in existence. We sent at once for a tuner and had it put into good condition."

The piano was bought by Signora Martelli's father, about 1819, from the Grand Ducal Palace at Siena, at an auction sale, held by order of the Minister of the Household, of all such things as he considered worthless and of no use. The piano was shuffled out of the Ducal Palace, much as some of our interesting relics have been shuffled out of the White House, and offered at auction.

The Christofori piano has a case of cedar, which is painted black on the outside. It stands on three clumsy turned legs. The keys are light-wood naturals and black sharps. The ivory knobs on the side blocks may be withdrawn, and the action removed from the case. There are two strings to each note, and the length of the instrument is seven feet seven and a half inches. It is three feet three inches wide at the front and nine and a half inches deep.

Keyed instruments at first found little favor in the ears of the Italians, who much preferred the violin with its "singing voice" and its superior capacity for expression. Yet they contributed much to the early history of this branch of the art, though the Germans cultivated more highly these instruments, which were, in their first state, very defective in producing melody. It was Domenico Scarlatti who laid the foundation of modern music for keyed instruments, and his music for the harpsichord was not confined to fugues and fantasias, as was most of the harpsichord music of early times. The real centre, however, in the line of progress for music for this instrument proved to be Germany, and Graun, Hasse, and John Christian Bach all wrote for the harpsichord.

Spinet

125

In America some of the first instruments to come into use were small organs. They are mentioned as early as 1711. Although large church organs, with three rows of keys and pedals, were in use in Europe by the opening of the sixteenth century, it was long before they were found here.

The rivalry which church music seems to inspire in the breasts of those who render it has long existed, and extends even to those who make the instruments. The following story from "Hawkin's History of Music" bears out this statement.

"Bernard Smith, or more properly Schmidt, a native of Germany, came to England with his nephews Gerard and Bernard, and to distinguish him from them obtained the name of 'Father Smith.' He was the rival of Harris from France and built an organ at Whitehall too precipitately, to gain the start of them, as they had arrived nearly at the same time in England. Emulation was powerfully exerted. Dallans joined Smith, but died in 1672, and Renatus Harris, son of the elder Harris, made great improvements. The contest became still warmer. The citizens of London, profiting by the rivalship of these excellent artists, erected organs in their churches; and the city, the court, and even the lawyers were divided in judgment as to the superiority. In order to decide the matter, the famous contest took place in the Temple Church upon their respective organs, played by eminent performers, before eminent judges, one of whom was the too celebrated Jeffreys. Blow & Purcell played for Smith, and Lully, organist to Queen Catharine, for Harris. In the course of the contest Harris challenged Father Smith to make, by a given time, the additional stops of the vox humana, the cremona or viol stop, the double courtel or bass flute, etc., which was accepted, and each exerted his abilities to the utmost. Jeffreys at length decided in favor of Smith, and Harris's organ was withdrawn. Father Smith maintained his reputation and was appointed organ-builder to Queen Anne. Harris went to Bristol."

In the first half of the eighteenth century the salaries paid to organists were small indeed, and it was customary for them to add to their modest stipend in various ways. In Charleston, S. C., in 1739, the organist taught the art of psalmody. A dozen years before this the organist at King's Chapel, Boston, Mass., taught dancing.

Mr. Drake, in his "History of Boston," says that King's Chapel was enlarged and rebuilt in 1713, and an organ was presented by Mr. Thomas Brattle. In 1756 the King's Chapel Society imported a new organ from London, and the old one was sold to St. Paul's Church, Newburyport. It was used there for eighty years, and then sold to St. John's Church, Portsmouth, N. H. The original pipes and wind-chest remain to-day in perfect condition.

The second church organ in New England was one in a case of English oak, presented by Bishop Berkeley to Trinity Church, Newport, R. I., in 1733. It had twenty-three gilded pipes and was fourteen and a half feet high, eight feet front, and eight feet deep. It was made by Richard Bridge, London. This organ was used for a hundred and eleven years by Trinity Church, till 1844, and after a sojourn of a few years in Brooklyn, N. Y., it was bought for a church in Portsmouth, R. I., where it still is, in excellent condition.

South Carolina, with her riches and her close communication with England, had abundant masters to teach not only the more elementary branches, but accomplishments as well. By 1774 there were two hundred persons in the colony engaged in teaching, and according to advertisements a knowledge of English, Latin, and Greek could be obtained at any time after 1712. French and music were constantly taught after 1733. Lessons on the harpsichord, spinet, violin, violoncello, guitar, and flute were all to be had after 1733, and the boys could be perfected in fencing and the girls in needlework before the middle of the century. By 1734 a dancing-school was opened at Charleston, and in 1760 Nicholas Valois gives notice that he still receives pupils in dancing, and that he has received "40 of the newest country dances, jiggs, rigadoons, etc., from London, which he proposes to teach."

In 1752 the vestry of St. Phillip's Church, Charleston, sent to London for an organist. The parish guaranteed him £50 sterling. He was to have the privilege of teaching the harpsichord or spinet, which would add 150 guineas more per annum, and also to have "benefits of concerts which his obliging behaviour to the gentlemen and ladies of the place may amount to 300 or 400 guineas

Harpsichord

more." The years between 1728 and 1763 were a time of unprecedented prosperity in South Carolina. The luxuries of the day were within reach of modest fortunes, and British modes and manners were eagerly followed. Josiah Quincy, in describing his visit to "Charles Town" in 1774, speaks of the famous St. Cecilia Society, which began as a musical club, all the performers being amateurs. He writes:

"The music was good, the two bass viols and French horns were grand. There were upwards of two hundred and fifty ladies present and it was called no great number. In loftiness of head-dress these ladies stoop to the daughters of the North; in richness of dress surpass them. The gentlemen, many of them dressed with richness and elegance—uncommon with us; many with swords on."

The Carolinians travelled often to England. They were lively and expensive in their dress, and an Englishman visiting Charleston in 1782 writes home that it "was the pleasantest and politest as it is one of the richest cities in all America." The charming old city still retains its two first recommendations, though, alas, the riches have flown. In 1768 the church organ pictured was imported from England for St. Michael's Church, Charleston. Within a little frame on one side of the organ is an inscription as follows:

JNO SNETZLER FECIT, LONDONI, 1767.

This inscription was found on one of the pipes of the organ when it was taken down during the bombardment of Charleston in the Civil War. At this time the organ was stored away in the Sunday-school room of St. Paul's Church, Radcliffeboro, for safe keeping. This is said to be the largest old church organ in the country, and this church probably had the first surpliced choir of boys. They are mentioned in the vestry books as early as 1794. The photograph of this organ was procured through the courtesy of Mr. Charles N. Beesley, of Charleston.

In the homes in various parts of the country, besides the virginal, were found the hand lyre, large and small fiddle, the recorder, flute, and hautboy. Some of these were imported, some were home-made. The first church organ built in New England was made for Christ

Cristofori Piano

Church, Boston, by Thomas Johnson, in 1752, and indeed by this time music in churches was pretty general all over the country. The puritans, with their hatred of anything secular, or, as it seems now, of anything that could ornament or beautify this none too joyous stay on earth, condemned music. In his "History of Music in New England", Mr. Hood says that before 1690 music was mostly written in psalm-books, the number of tunes rarely exceeding five or six. At the beginning of the eighteenth century New England congregations were rarely able to sing more than three or four tunes, and even these were sung by the doleful process of "lining out". The deacon would read one line of a psalm, and the congregation would sing it. Then he would read the next, and so on. About 1720 an effort was made to improve this method of singing, but it met with violent opposition. Some of the objections advanced were that "it grieved good men and caused them to behave disorderly;" that it was "Quakerish and Popish"; that "the names of the notes were blasphemous;" etc. Yet after a while the congregations were soothed by the publication of several "Letters of Pacification", written by ministers, and some books were published like that of the Rev. Thomas Walter of Roxbury, Mass., entitled:

"The Grounds and Rules of Musick Explained. Or, An Introduction to the Art of Singing by Note Fitted to the Meanest Capacity By Thomas Walter, A.M. Recommended by Several Ministers, 'Let everything that hath truth praise the Lord.' Ps. 150. 6. Boston."

Singing-Schools for the instruction of the young were opened, and music, the only science allowed, crept into the church. "The Newport Mercury" for January 8, 1770, contains the following:

"The Public are hereby informed That a Singing-School will be opened at Mr. Bradford's Schoolhouse next Thursday evening by a Person who has taught the various Branches of Psalmody in the Provinces of New York, Massachusetts Bay and Connecticut and those Gentlemen and Ladies who have an inclination to improve in this Excellent Art may expect all that Care and Dilligence which is necessary to their being rightly instructed in the same."

William Tuckey of New York was a schoolmaster in that city about 1753, and taught singing to children. In 1766 the trustees of Trinity Church paid him £15 for performing the music for the opening of St. Paul's Chapel in New York.

By 1775 choir singing had become more general, and the old system of lining out was dying, but dying hard. In several parishes the singers, male and female, were requested to sit in the gallery and "carry on the singing in public worship." Many anecdotes are given in Dr. Ritter's "Music in America", showing how the choir, once called into being, soon became a thorn in the ministers flesh, sometimes being rebuked from the pulpit, and in retaliation refusing to sing.

Harp - Image: Shriram Rajagopalan

That the music was bad goes without saying, for the singers were ill-trained under incompetent teachers, and the music was often incorrect. Dr. Ritter gives the proportion of women voices to men as about twenty to one hundred and thirteen. The proposition to let women sing the air was not to be considered for a moment, since men had a "prescriptive right to lead, and women were forbidden to take the first part in song or any other religious service."

S. Howe published in 1804 the "Farmer's Evening Entertainment", and in it gives directions for beating time:

"To beat crotchets in common Time, let the fingers fall on the table six inches, then bring the heel of the hand down gently, then raising it a little higher, throw

129

open the fingers to begin the next bar. For triple Time, let the fingers fall on the table, then the heel of the hand, then raise the whole hand six inches, keeping the fingers straight, which fills the bar."

But while religious music was undergoing violent changes, secular music was having a more peaceful time, and instrument-builders were becoming more numerous and successful. In 1774, in the "New York Gazette" is this advertisement.

"John Shybli, Organ-builder at Mr. Samuel Princes' Cabinet-makers in Horse-and-Cart St. New York. Makes, repairs and tunes all sorts of organs, harpsichords and Fortepianos, on the most reasonable terms. N. B. He has now ready for sale one neat chamber organ, one hammer spinet, one common spinet.

Mr. Samuel Blyth of Salem, Mass., made "spinnetts" (they spelled them with two n's in those days) and then gave instruction upon them. He did not require cash payment either, as witness the following bill, now in the possession of Mr. Henry Brooks, author of "Olden-Time Music."

Mrs. Margaret Barton to Sam Blyth Dr.			
To making a spinnett for her daughter			
Supra Cr.	£18	0	0
By 34 oz 1¾ dwt of Old silver a. 6. pr. oz.	£10	4	11
By cash to Ballance	£7	15	1
	£18	0	0.

Salem 7th Feb'y 1786
Rec'd payment
Saml Blyth

At Mount Vernon is still to be seen the harpsichord bought for Nellie Custis by General Washington. In 1798, writing to a young friend at Philadelphia, she says:

"I am not very industrious, but I work a little, read a little, play on the harpsichord, and find my time fully taken up with daily employments."

There is an old song given in "Historic Landmarks of Maryland and Virginia" as being one which Nellie Custis used to sing, accompanying herself on the harpsichord. We wonder who selected for her.

"THE TRAVELER AT THE WIDOW'S GATE.
"A traveler stop't at a widow's Gate,She kept an Inn and he wanted to bait; She kept an Inn and he wanted to bait;But the widow she slighted her guest,But the widow she slighted her guest,For when nature was forming an ugly race,She certainly moulded the traveler's faceAs a sample for all the rest, as a sample for all the rest.The chambermaid's sides they were ready to crackWhen she saw his queer nose and the hump on his back;A hump isn't handsome, no doubt;And though t'is

confessed the prejudice goesVery strongly in favor of wearing a nose,A nose shouldn't look like a snout.A bag full of gold on the table he laid,'T had a wondrous effect on the widow and maid,And they quickly grew marvelous civil;The money immediately altered the case,They were charmed with his hump and his snout and his face,Though he still might have frightened the devil.He paid like a prince, gave the widow a smack,And flop'd on his horse at the door like a sack,While the landlady, touching his chin,Said, 'Sir, should you travel this country again,I heartily hope that the sweetest of menWill stop at the widow's to drink.'"

The names of some other popular songs of this period were "The White Cockade," "Irish Howl," "Hessian Camp," "Nancy of the Mill," "Every Inch a Soldier," "When Nichola First to Court Began," "Baron Steuben's March," "Sweet Village of the Valley," "King of Sweden's March," etc. The Revolutionary echoes seemed to be still reverberating.

In the "Domestic Life of Thomas Jefferson" there is a description given of Monticello, which he built in 1770-1772, and a diagram of the lower rooms showing where each piece of furniture stood. It seems very sparsely fitted out, yet it had a great reputation for elegance. The house was but a story and a half high, and on the ground floor was a great

Bass Viol

hall, drawing-room, dining-room, tea-room, sitting-room, and two bedrooms besides the one occupied by Jefferson himself. In this latter room was a couch upon which Jefferson rested when studying, a dressing-table and mirror, a chair near the wall, and beside it a small bookcase. There was no closet, so in one corner was a rack upon which his clothes where hung. The chief ornament to the drawing-room was his daughter's, Mrs. Randolph's, harpsichord. Standing about were many busts, of Alexander of Russia, Hamilton, Voltaire, Turgot, and Napoleon, and portraits of Washington, Adams, Franklin, Madison, etc. The house was at least abundantly furnished with chairs, for Jefferson himself leaves an inventory which states that there were 36 of mahogany and 44 of gold leaf. Of small tea and card tables there were 13. In the dining-room, well toward its centre, stood Jefferson's chair and a candle-stand. His particular hobby was blooded horses, and he used only the finest Virginia stock.

This same harpsichord was, as early as 1785, in Jefferson's thoughts, and he writes to his daughter, Polly, from France, that she shall be taught to play on it, as well as to draw and dance, to read and talk French, "and such other things as will make you more worthy of the love of your friends." Even in remote places like Monticello, where everything had to be transported by cart, or at Johnson Hall, Sir

John Johnson's home in the Mohawk valley, harpsichords, as well as other expensive luxuries, were to be found. Sir John's harpsichord was confiscated by the government in December, 1777, at the same time with the table which is now at the Historical Rooms in Albany. While musical instruments are only rarely mentioned in the inventories of the great body of the people, yet we have seen that they were here both of domestic manufacture and imported. Thomas Harrison, organist of Trinity Church, advertises in the "New York Mercury" for 1761 that he has "harpsichords and spinets imported and for sale."

The harp was not so often seen as other instruments, on account both of the great cost of the instrument and of the difficulty of tuning it. It was not until 1720 that the pedal harp was invented by a Bavarian named Hochbrücker. By means of the pedal working a small plate set with projecting pins, the performer was able to raise the pitch of each string a semitone. The mechanism was concealed in the front pillar, and each note was affected in all its octaves. Erard made farther improvements. The harp shown is in the Metropolitan Museum, New York. It is a very handsome one,

Glass Harmonica

painted blue, and resting on four claw feet. The pillar is fluted, and the ornaments, three medallions of dancing girls, with wreaths below, are executed in brass. It has forty-two strings of gut and seven pedals. It was made by Naderman, Paris, France, late in the eighteenth century. Naderman perfected the action of the first pedal harp invented by Hochbrücker. In the South Kensington Museum, London, England, is a harp which belonged to the ill-fated Marie Antoinette; it also was made by Naderman in 1780.

The harp in its various forms is an instrument of great antiquity. The Greeks and Romans, ever alive to the possibilities of everything that tended to grace and beauty, admired this instrument not only for its sweet sound but for its pleasing form. We must look to Egypt for the origin of the harp, as there are representations in their picture writings of stringed instruments of a bow-form that support the idea that the first conception of a harp was drawn from the tense string of a warrior's bow. This very primitive instrument was borne on the performer's shoulder and played horizontally.

Between this crude instrument and the splendid vertical harps shown in the frescoes of the time of Rameses III., painted more than three thousand years ago, there is a chain of pictures showing so many varieties of forms that the growth from the bow-form into the triangular harp is explained. The Assyrians, like the Egyptians, had harps without a front pillar, but differing from them in using sound-holes, and having the sound body uppermost. We assign to King David the harp, but mediæval artists more frequently depicted him with the psaltery, a horizontal stringed instrument, the parent of the piano.

The harp has always been the instrument of the Celtic race, and harpists were held in peculiar veneration. For many a long year harpists traveled from one castle to another, sure always of a welcome and seat in a warm corner. In return they not only amused the company with their songs, but brought the news, and isolated and remote families often heard from the outer world by such uncertain means as these. For centuries the English harpers were protected in many ways, and no one has taken advantage of such a picturesque class with the skill of Sir Walter Scott. The most renowned one he introduced as a character was Blondel de Nesle, in the "Talisman," that wonderful picture of the days of the Crusades. The first greeting to the youth when he appeared at Richard's camp shows the estimation in which these knights of the harp were held.

"Blondel de Nesle!" Richard exclaimed joyfully "welcome from Cyprus, my king of minstrels! Welcome to the King of England, who rates not his own dignity more highly than he does thine.... And what news, my gentle master, from the land of the lyre? Anything fresh from the trouveurs of Provence? Anything from the minstrels of merry Normandy? Above all, hast thou thyself been busy?"

It is also said that Richard Cœur de Lion's place of confinement in Germany on his return from the Holy Land was discovered when Blondel sung beneath the Tower Tenebreuse a tenson which they had jointly composed, and to which the king replied.

Edward I. and his Queen were fond of music and encouraged musicians, as the following entries in their accounts of the household expenditures show:

"To Melioro, the harper of Sir John Mantravers, for playing on the harp when the king was bled, twenty shillings; likewise to Walter Luvel, the harper of Chichester, whom the King found playing on his harp before the tomb of St. Richard at Chichester Cathedral, six shillings and eight pence."

Henry V. was a performer on the harp at an early age, and his wife, Catherine of Valois, shared his taste, as an entry in the Issue Rolls reads:

"By the hands of William Menston was paid £8 13s 4d, for two new harps purchased for King Henry and Queen Catherine."

These harps were tuned with a key like the more modern instruments, and the player improvised his words to suit the taste of the company in which he found himself. Harpists were employed much at courts, and in 1666 Pepys says that for want of pay to the household—

—"many of the musique are ready to starve, they being five years behind hand for wages; nay, Evens, the famous man upon the Harp, having not his equal in the world, did the other day die for mere want, and was fain to be buried at the almes of the parish, and carried to his grave in the dark at night without one linke, but that Mr. Hingston met it by chance, and did give 12*d.* to buy two or three links."

At the present day, though at no instrument does a graceful woman look more graceful, solo performers are very rare; but in the orchestra the harp has an important place on account of its tone, such composers as Gounod, Berlioz, Liszt, and Wagner using it freely in their scores. In this country there are only occasional references in the old papers to it, and an advertisement by Signor Pucci in 1815 that he gives concerts on the "Fashionable and much admired King David's Pedal Harp", seems to be an effort to introduce it to the notice of music-lovers of the day.

Madame Malibran, who achieved such a success in opera in New York about 1825, used to accompany herself on the harp when she sang in response to an encore. But it can never be considered a popular instrument.

Geib Piano

In Dwight's "History of Music in Boston", he says that at the beginning of the nineteenth century the population of Boston numbered about six thousand families, and that not fifty pianos could be found. Only a few of Boston's churches had organs, while those in country parishes were, almost without exception, without them. The use of instruments had crept slowly into the choir, and if they had a flute and a bass viol they considered they did well. Very often a clarinet usurped the place of the flute. The bass viol was, however, the most popular instrument, and when, some years later, concerts began to be given, and musical societies formed, the bass viol was lugged about, notwithstanding its ponderous size, and duly performed its part in the accompaniment.

The bass viol shown earlier is an interesting one. It was made by Deacon Justin Hitchcock, and used by him in the choir of the Congregational Church, Deerfield, Mass., in 1778. Both it and the pitch-pipe used by him as leader of the choir are now resting silent in Memorial Hall. Deacon Justin did not confine his musical performances to psalmody and the accompanying of hymns. Like all the Deerfield men of that day he was a fighter, as who should not be who was brought up among those silent hills which had seen so much of "ye barbarous enemy" and knew the tales of French invasion? The stories of warfare and captivity were still fresh in the minds of the people of Deerfield when Deacon Justin responded to the Lexington alarm. His fife it was that inspired the weary Deerfield minute-men to press on to

134

Boston to meet the British. Nor was this the only campaign in which he played a part, for he never wearied of displaying the trophies captured after the disastrous experience of Burgoyne, when, harassed and in flight, he abandoned his baggage.

A very similar bass-viol, but of German manufacture, was played during the latter part of the eighteenth century in a church in Stonington, Connecticut. The sisters of the Hospital General in Montreal, before the conquest of Canada, imported several of these instruments from France for use in the convent choir. So they must have been played upon by women sometimes.

Nuns Piano

An instrument that is interesting rather than handsome is the glass harmonica pictured earlier. It has thirty-five bowls or glasses arranged on a central rod. Some of the glasses are now missing, but originally it had a compass of three octaves. The case is three feet nine and a half inches long, and one foot four and three quarters inches wide. The interest in this class of instruments arises from the fact that it was invented by Benjamin Franklin. It has about as much capacity for producing music as the "musical glasses". One of these latter instruments consists of twenty-four glasses closely resembling finger-bowls and standing in a wooden table-like case. They are partially filled with water, and the performer produces notes by rubbing on the rim with the finger. They were occasionally to be met with, and date about the first decade, possibly a little later, of the nineteenth century. There is one in a perfect condition in Rochester, N. Y. The case is of handsome mahogany, and the instrument belongs to Mrs. James McKown.

Up to 1760 pianos were made in the wing shape, like the harpsichords, but at that date a man named Zumpe made a square one. By 1800 there were a number of makers in New York, and they turned out many very handsome instruments. Astor, Broadwood, and Clementi were three great makers in London, and sent many pianos over here. There is a slender-legged, fragile, Clementi piano in Memorial Hall, Deerfield, which was given by a father to his daughter. The story still clings to it that he sold a house in order to buy it for her.

John Geib, and his sons, John H., Adam, and William, were among the best-known early makers of pianofortes. They opened a shop in Maiden Lane as early as 1807, and advertised not only pianos of their own manufacture, built on a new plan, but those of London makers as well. They held this shop in Maiden Lane, with a brief interruption of one year, till 1828, when W. Geib moved up to the

135

corner of 11th Street and Third Avenue. It was from this establishment that he sold the handsome piano shown earlier which is now at the Historical Rooms, Albany. The name-plate over the keyboard has the following inscription.

"W. GEIB, THIRD AVENUE, CORNER 11TH ST. NEW YORK. MANUFACTURER OF CABINET, GRAND, HARMONIC, AND SQUARE PIANO FORTES, CHURCH AND CHAMBER ORGANS."

This piano is mahogany inlaid, and has a handsome brass moulding and brass ornamental bands at the tops of the legs. It has six legs and a pedal, and the top of the lid has a small rest for the music. The stool, very richly carved with pillar and claw feet, belongs to an earlier period than the piano, this shape dating from about 1810-20.

Indeed, from its ornamentation, the stool would seem to go more fittingly with the very elegant piano shown earlier. This is of rosewood, and was made by Robert and William Nuns, and sold by Du Bois and Stodard, New York. It was probably made about 1823-25, for

Upright Piano

in pattern of carving, moulding, drawers for music, etc., it is very similar to the pianos made at this time by the Geib Brothers. At the top of each leg is a richly engraved band of brass, and rosette, to conceal the place where the pin held the leg to the instrument. The drawer knobs were doubtless brass also, for these are not the original ones.

The panel above the keyboard is beautifully painted in metallic lustre, and has two carved panels besides, over velvet. The legs are boldly carved with the acanthus leaf, and everything about the piano is as elegant as possible. By the time these last two instruments were made music had taken a decided advance. Musical societies were organized in all the large cities; there were the Handel and Haydn Society; the New York Philharmonic Society; the New York Choral Society; Beethoven Society of Portland, Maine; Philadelphia Musical Fund; Harmonic Society of Baltimore, and equally flourishing musical organizations in several cities of the South, notably New Orleans and Charleston.

Music-dealers all over the country advertised their wares; there were instruction-books and sheet music to be had:—

136

—"Overtures, battles, sonatas, duets for four hands, airs with variations, rondos, songs, glees, catches, sacred songs, original Scotch airs, little ballads, marches, waltzes, dances, and Mozart's songs."

In view of the selection of good music that could be obtained, it is amusing to know how popular were such ditties as "Mary's Tears," "Apollo, thy Treasure," and "Sweet Little Ann," written by Shaw, the blind singer of Providence. They seem hardly an advance upon "Bid Me, When Forty Winters," "Little Sally's Wooden Ware," and the "Comic Irish song 'Boston News'" which were used as concert selections a quarter of a century earlier.

In the image on the previous page is an upright piano made by Julius Fiot, Philadelphia, in 1827. The heavy veneered Empire curved posts are noticeable, and an extra old-fashioned appearance is given to it by the movable candle-brackets fastened to either side. In the upper part were little silk curtains to cover the mechanism, and their arrangement does not seem to have been particularly neat. This was a very early example of the upright shape, and is now in Memorial Hall, Philadelphia.

Antique Clocks

CONTRIVANCES for the measurement of time are of such antiquity that the first such implement is wrapped in the mysteries of a forgotten past. Before any mechanical form had been invented by which the rate of motion of a staff or pointer was made to indicate the lapse of time, the shadow of the sun in his apparent daily progress was used to mark the passing hours. A gnomon or pin erected so as to throw its traveling shadow across a graduated arc constitutes a dial. This was the earliest form.

The subject of sun-dials has been most exhaustively treated by Mrs. Gatty in her "Book of Sun-Dials", and later in our own country by Mrs. Earle. In England and Scotland many dials may still be found standing in old-fashioned gardens where they have marked the flight of time for hundreds of years. Many more dials, vertical ones, are to be found on the walls of public buildings, sometimes on churches, and on country houses as well. Not only stationary dials, but portable ones also, of silver and gold, were made and were long in use. Some of these are to be seen in various museums over the country, but most of them seem to have disappeared. George Washington owned a portable dial, and had a stationary one placed near his front door at Mt. Vernon.

In some of the famous old gardens of the South that still survive, echoes of their former glory, the sun-dial yet holds its accustomed place. In the very heart of New York city there is to-day a sun-dial; not one person in a hundred that passes knows that it is there, nor would scarcely one person in fifty know what it was. It stands on the lawn of Grace Church rectory, on Broadway, near Tenth Street. This spot of green in a wilderness of brick and stone refreshes the eye of many a hurrying pedestrian, and the dial marks the flight of the hours as sharply as if it stood in a country wilderness, amid birds and flowers.

The sun-dial was an important part of every great garden in early times. One was set up at Whitehall, England, in the sixteenth century.

"In a garden joining to this palace there is a Jet d'eau, with a sun-dial, which, while strangers looking at, a quantity of water forced by a wheel, which the gardiner turns at a distance, through a number of little pipes, plentifully sprinkles those that are standing around."

William Lawson, writing in 1618 a book on "A New Orchard and Garden", gives the directions about laying it out.

"And in some corner (or more) a true Dyall or clock, and some Anticke works, and especially silver sounding Musique, mixt instruments and voyces, gracing all the rest; How will you be rapt with delight?"

In 1821 William Cobbett wrote his "Rural Rides". In one of them he discourses of a visit to Moor Park, once the seat of Sir William Temple, whose heart, enclosed in a silver box, was said to have been buried in 1698 beneath his sun-dial. But Cobbett casts a doubt upon this time-honored legend by declaring that it was beneath a garden seat that the silver box was buried. Charles Lamb, in his essay "The Old Benchers of the Inner Temple", discourses lovingly of the sun-dial. "It spoke of moderate labours, of pleasures not protracted after sunset, of temperance, and good hours." The dials made out of herbs and flowers come in for a special share of his commendation. How much more the dial induces meditation than the clock, but how very much lost we should be, these bustling times, if we had to depend upon one of these delightful but irresponsible "antiques" which say to you quite distinctly, "I mark only sunny hours."

In an inventory of the property of William Bennett, East Greenwich, Rhode Island, who died in 1753, among other articles were mentioned "warming-pan, pewter, sun-dial, book, debts, £10."

After the dial came the clepsydra, a sort of clock, which measured time by the graduated flow of some liquid, like water, through a small aperture. While the hour-glass was not known in England till 886, it had been used in Rome long before; but inventions traveled slowly in those days. The hour-glass remained long in use, even after the invention of clocks, and while we know it chiefly as marking the period of

Tall Case Clocks, English. Daniel Quare - maker, 1690. J. Harrison, maker, 1715.

agony of some unwilling victim at the piano, it was used even later than the noon mark on the window-ledge, which may be seen to-day on some of the old houses still standing.

A writer in the "Gentlemen's Magazine" for 1746 says that he was present on an occasion when a grave-digger was at work in Clerkenwell Fields.

"He had dug pretty deep, and was come to a coffin which had lain so long that it was quite rotten, and the plate so eaten with rust that he could not read anything of the inscription. In clearing away the old wood the grave-digger found an hour-glass close to the left side of the skull, with sand still in it. Being a lover of

139

antiquity, I bought it of him, and have since learned from some antiquarians that it was an ancient custom to put an hour-glass in the coffin to show that the sands of life were run."

The origin of clockwork is involved in great obscurity, though there are statements by many writers that clocks were in use as early as the ninth century.

By 1288 a clock was placed in the Old Palace Yard, London, and remained there till the reign of Queen Elizabeth. In 1292 a clock was placed on Canterbury Cathedral, and in 1368 a striking clock was erected at Westminster. By 1500, clocks were used in private houses, and watches were introduced. In 1368 three Dutch clockmakers were invited to come to England to teach the business to native workers, though "Dutch clocks" and their makers were held in contempt some years later.

There was a clock put into the tower of Hampton Court Palace in 1540 by a maker whose initials were "N. O.", all that posterity knows of him. It was the oldest clock in England that kept fairly good time. In 1575 George Gaver, "serjeant painter" as his title runs, had a sum of money allowed him for "painting the great dial at Hampton Court Palace, containing hours of day and night, and the course of sun and moon." In 1649 a striking part was added. By 1711 it was found that the clock had not been running as correctly as it should, owing to the fact that some careless or ignorant workman had removed some important parts of the works. After this discovery it was left neglected for many years, and finally lost its hands. It was in this condition in the first quarter of the nineteenth century, when G. P. R. James wrote a poem entitled "Old Clock Without Hands at Hampton Court."

In 1835 the old works were removed, and a set of works put in which had been made in 1690 by Villiamy, for a clock in the Queen's Palace, St. James' Park. As this clock was not powerful enough to drive the astronomical works, these were put away. In 1880 this old clock was also removed, sold for old brass, and a brand-new clock substituted. It seems a pity that one of the earliest clocks known should have been destroyed. It was not till 1639 that Galileo published his discovery of the isochronous property of the pendulum, which was eight years after the incorporation of the London Clockmakers Company. Not only did this company train workers for clockmaking, but they also inspected clocks brought into England, and rejected those which they deemed unworthy.

Richard Harris is said to have been the man who first connected the pendulum with clockwork movement, about 1641, and Harris's method was improved by Huyghens, so that by 1658 very trustworthy time-keepers were in use. Mr. Lockwood in his book on "Colonial Furniture," says that the first clock mentioned in the Massachusetts Colony was found in Boston in 1638, but in Lechford's note-book it is said that Joseph Stratton had of his brother in 1628 a clock and a watch. In 1640 Henry Parks, of Hartford, left a clock by will to the church. The first clock in New Haven belonged to John Davenport, who died in 1670.

E. Needham, of Lynn, Mass., died in 1677. She left an estate valued at £1,117. The barn, land, out-houses and dwelling house were valued at £400. This included a "range of ston wall fensing." Her silver watch, spoons, and other plate were worth £5. She had a striking clock, another watch, and a "larum that does not strike." These early clocks were probably like the ones shown on the following page. They were called "lantern," "chamber", or "birdcage" clocks. The lantern clock shown is of the pattern known as the "dolphin fret," on account of the ornamentation above the dial, which is made by two dolphins with crossed tails.

This clock was made by Thomas Tompion, of London, a famous maker, who lived in the last half of the seventeenth century and died in 1713. He was clockmaker to Charles II., and was held in high esteem, as may be gathered from the fact that he was buried in Westminster Abbey, where his tomb may still be seen.

Tompion was called the "Father of English Clockmaking", and has left a more enduring fame than any of his contemporaries. He had been a blacksmith, and before his time watches as well as clocks had been of

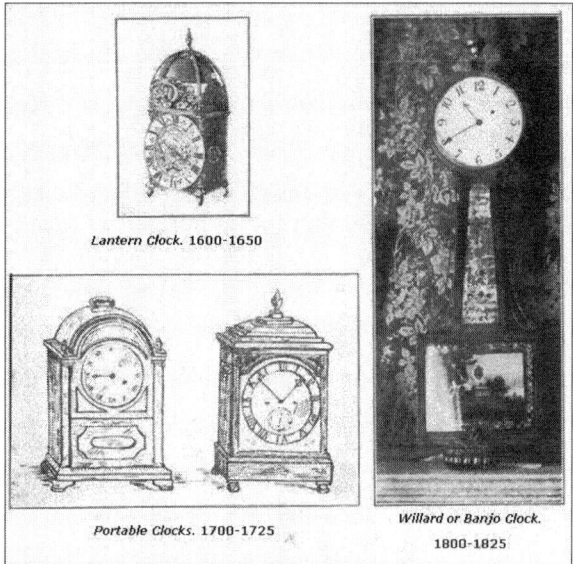

Lantern Clock. 1600-1650

Portable Clocks. 1700-1725

Willard or Banjo Clock. 1800-1825

Three Centuries of Clocks

rude construction, and the watch of Charles I., which is still preserved, has a catgut string instead of a chain. Indeed watches of that construction were in use for a long time after the chain was invented. Very curiously, through some of the strange chances which govern inanimate as well as animate things, this very watch has found at least a temporary home in this country.

When Oliver Cromwell obtained his great victory over Charles II., and drove the enemy from hedge to hedge till they finally took refuge in the city of Worcester, there were seven thousand prisoners and great spoils, among the latter the royal carriage in which the king had been carried. In the carriage was this watch, which was used by Charles II. as it had been by his father Charles I. It had been made for the latter in 1640, and after more than two centuries of vicissitudes still ticks bravely on. It is of the earliest pattern of watches, made entirely by hand and of great size, as it measures four and a half inches in diameter, and is an inch and a half thick. The case is very handsome, of pierced silver in a pattern of flowers and leaves, and has three winding-holes on the back,—one for winding the works, one for the alarm, and one for the striking attachment, which consists of a small silver bell within the perforated case. It has but one hand to mark the time and goes thirty-six hours. There is an outer case into which the watch may be slipped, made of copper with a leather cover studded with silver.

The watch was kept by Cromwell himself for many years, but after the Restoration it fell into the hands of Joseph Kipling, of Overstone House, North Hants, England, a relative of Rudyard Kipling. Joseph Kipling was also an ancestor of Mr. Wilfred Powell, British consul at the port of Philadelphia, and present owner of the watch.

Robert Hooker invented the double balance in 1658, and Tompion completed it in 1675, and made a watch which he presented to Charles II. Two others were made and sent to the Dauphin of France, where Huyghens had obtained a patent for spiral-spring watches. This idea was not original with him, but was obtained from a man named Oldenburg. It is allowed, however, that it is Huyghens who first made those watches which went without strings or chains. Barlow, in the reign of James II. is said to have discovered the method of making striking watches, but, Quare's being judged superior by the Privy Council, Barlow did not get a patent.

Tompion's watches were in great demand for a long time, owing to their being large and well made, the wheels being of well-hammered brass. Three most eminent watchmakers of this time were Tompion, who died in 1713; Daniel Quare, who succeeded him and died in 1725; and George Graham, who followed Quare and died in 1775. They all belonged to the Society of Friends.

Watches cannot claim the antiquity of clocks, but they can be traced as far back as the fourteenth century. In shape they were like an egg, and Nuremburg claims their earliest manufacture. Although it is said that they were introduced into England in 1577, yet it is certain that Henry VIII. had a watch, and in 1572 the Earl of Leicester presented to Queen Elizabeth—

—"one amlet or shakell of golde, all over fairly garnished with small diamandes, and fower and one smaller pieces, fully garnished with like diamandes and hanging thereat a round clocke fullie garnished with diamandes and an appendant hanging thereat."

They were so unusual that they were worn ostentatiously round the neck hanging to a chain.

In an old play called "A Mad World, My Masters!", one of the characters says "Ah, by my troth, sir, besides a jewel and a jewel's fellow, a good fair watch that hung about my neck." When Malvolio was telling over the agreeable ways in which he would occupy himself after his marriage with Olivia, he says, "I frown the while, and perchance wind up my watch or play with some rich jewel." Watches called "strikers" were known in Ben Jonson's time, for he says in his "Staple of News"

"'T strikes! One, two,
Three, four, five, six. Enough, enough, dear watch.
Thy pulse hath beat enough. Now stop and rest."

Watches were in use so rarely in the early times of James I. that it was deemed a cause of suspicion when in 1605 one was found upon the person of Guy Vaux. By 1638 they were more common, and in a comedy of that year called "The Antipodes" it is complained that—

"—every clerk can carry
The time of day in his pocket."

The prices of these first time-keepers must have been high, but there are no records of them left. In 1643 the sum of £4 was paid to redeem a watch taken from a nobleman in battle. In 1661 there was advertised as lost—

—"a round watch of reasonable size, showing the day of the month, age of the moon, and tides, upon the upper plate. Thomas Alcock fecit."

The redoubtable Pepys's curiosity extended to watches, and he writes in his diary, December 22, 1665:

"I to my Lord Brouncker's, and there spent the evening by my desire in seeing his Lordship open to pieces and make up again his watch, thereby being taught what I never knew before; and it is a thing very well worth my having seen, and am mightily pleased and satisfied with it."

The English became such famous watchmakers that in 1698 an act was passed to compel makers to place their names upon those they made, in order that discreditable ones might not be passed for English. Among the possessions of the English Crown is a watch which was found about 1770 in Bruce Castle, Scotland. On the dial plate is written "Robertus B. Rex Scotorum", and over the face is a shield of convex horn instead of glass. Robert Bruce began his reign in 1305 and died in 1328, long before watches were supposed to be known in England. The case of this watch is of silver in a raised pattern on a ground of blue enamel.

Striking watches were highly esteemed. When Sarah, Duchess of Marlborough died in 1744 she left a will covering six skins of parchment, and she designated the disposal of "manors, parsonages, rectories, advowsons, messuages, lands, tenements, tithes, and hereditaments", in half a dozen counties. She also specified many of her jewels, and among them is her "striking watch which formerly belonged to Lady Sutherland."

The lantern style of clock before mentioned was not original with Tompion, but had been used in England from the beginning of the seventeenth century. They ran by weights, and the clock had to be affixed to a bracket or shelf in order to give room for the weights to hang. In the clock in the last image the cords and weights have been removed. The faces of these clocks always stood out beyond the frame, and were of beautifully engraved or etched brass, as may be seen in the figure. The single hand showed only the fifths of the hour and the hours. The small dial in the centre was to set the alarm, which struck the bell, but in some of them the hours were struck also.

The portable or table clock came into use early in 1600, and one of them shown in the last image, with the oval top to the dial which was not in use till the last part of the seventeenth century. These were the common house clocks of the period and were easily carried about. Some found their way to America, and as they were well made, with brass works, they are still able to give correct time. This style of clock was made for many years, and was manufactured in substantially the same way, late in the eighteenth century, by such famous makers as Isaac Fox and Joseph Rose.

Samuel Pepys, who recorded everything that was going on in London, in July 28th, 1660, has this entry.

"To Westminster, and there met Mr. Henson, who had formerly had the brave clock that went with bullets, (which is now taken away from him by the King, it being his goods)."

In the "Gentlemen's Magazine" for 1785 is the following comment on this statement of Pepys.

"Some clocks are still made with a small ball, or bullet on an inclined plane, which turns every minute."

The King's clocks probably dropped bullets. Gainsborough, the painter, had a brother who was a dissenting minister at Henley-on-Thames and possessed a strong genius for mechanics. He invented a clock of very peculiar construction, which after his death was deposited in the British Museum. It told the hour by a little bell, and was kept in motion by a leaden bullet which dropped, from a spiral reservoir at the top of the clock, into a little ivory bucket. This was so contrived as to discharge it at the bottom, and by means of a counterweight was carried up to the top of the clock, where it received another bullet, which was discharged as the former. This seems to have been an attempt at perpetual motion.

Catherine of Braganza was responsible for introducing many luxuries to the English world. Pepys makes this mention of her clock in 1664.

"Mr. Pierce showed me the Queen's [the Portuguese Princess, wife of Charles II] bed-chamber ... and her holy water at her head as she sleeps, with a clock by her bedside, wherein a lamp burns that tells her the time of the night at any time."

Pepys speaks again in 1667 of going to see—

—"a piece of clocke-worke made by an Englishman—indeed very good, wherein all the several states of man's age to one hundred years old, is shown very pretty and solemne."

Besides the dolphin fret shown on the Tompion clock in the last image there were other patterns, perhaps the earliest being what is called the "heraldic fret", which was a coat-of-arms with scroll-work on either side. This was not used after

1650, so any clocks bearing this pattern belong to the first half of the seventeenth century. It was early seen that to be accurate a clock must have some contrivance to keep it going while it is being wound. In the old-fashioned house clocks which were wound by merely pulling a string, and in which one such winding served both for the going and striking parts, this was done by using what was called the endless chain of Huyghens, which consists of a chain or string with ends joined together, passing over two pulleys which are placed on the arbors of the great wheels, and which have both spikes and deep grooves in them to prevent the chain from slipping off.

To the best clocks in England it was usual to apply the gridiron pendulum of Harrison or the mercurial pendulum of Graham. The length of the pendulum of most clocks made before 1800 was 39 inches; that is, after the long pendulum came into use at all. The earliest were called "bob pendulums", which swung so far at the sides that it was often necessary to cut slits in the sides of the case, if it was hung inside, for it was as frequently hung outside. Many clocks which started with bob pendulums were changed to those having long ones, which about 1680 came very much into fashion.

In Mr. Charles Britten's various books on clocks and clockmaking he has gathered together all the minute particulars which are obtainable on this subject, and which are of chief interest to collectors of clocks. Most people are content with one clock, particularly if it be of the "grandfather" variety.

The term "clock" was only applied to the bell upon which the hour was rung till well into the fourteenth century, and as late as the time of James I. clocks were known as horologes. Even at the present day the old term has clung to the church-tower time-piece in some of the least-traveled parts of England, and in the quaint and lovely little town of Wells the Cathedral clock is called the "horologe."

There are long-case clocks made by Tompion to be found in this country; for of course all the first clocks were of English make. The earliest long-case clocks were made by William Clement about 1680, and within the same year Tompion was making them too. The peculiarities of these first clocks are quite marked and easily distinguished, for the dials were square, and the top of the case lifted off to permit of winding.

An early and handsome specimen of such a clock is seen in the previous image. This clock was made in the latter part of the seventeenth century by Daniel Quare, the successor of Thomas Tompion. It is a one-year clock and is at Hampton Court Palace. The dial face is square, and the top lifts off. The case is very handsomely carved and has some very handsome figures on the top. The second tall case clock shown earlier is in a black and gold lacquered case, and was made by J. Harrison in 1715. It is at the Guildhall Museum, London. This shows the carved top of the dial face which became universally adopted. The most important part of one of these clocks is the pendulum, for the long case was brought into use solely for the pendulum, as mechanism had not been invented to permit it to swing in a confined

145

space. The first long-case clocks were comparatively small in size, and during the reign of William III., when everything Dutch was in fashion, the cases were ornamented with marquetry in beautiful patterns and variously coloured woods. Sometimes this was made even richer by inlay of mother-of-pearl, and there were cases also of splendid lacquer-work, gold on black grounds, like that earlier, some of which found their way to America and are either museum specimens or treasured in private collections. There are many clocks with English works housed in Dutch cases, but this is understandable from the fact that so many Dutch cabinet-makers were settled in London.

Besides the square face to the dial of these early clocks there were peculiarities of the case as well. On either side of the upper part of the case there were carved spiral pillars, like those we find in old chairs of the same period. These were occasionally finished off by carved or gilt pilasters, and on some choice specimens, notably of Tompion's clocks, there are pillars at the back also. This style of pillar was used also in Queen Anne's time. The clocks might stand flat on the floor or be raised an inch or two on a short foot. The long doors had mouldings, corresponding to the period of their manufacture, and many had a piece of glass or a bull's-eye let into the wood, so that the motion of the pendulum could be seen.

Some of the most distinguishing marks on these clocks are the hour circles. Before the minute hand came into use the double circles seen in the mantle clocks were in use. Between them the hour is divided into quarters, the half hour being shown by a longer stroke, or an ornament like a fleur-de-lys. When the minute hand came into use, besides the double circle containing the numerals denoting the hours, and the smaller figures showing the minutes, there were on the outer edge marks or divisions to denote the quarter hours, the device being a cross or a dagger. The dial faces were beautifully embellished with engraving, those of the William III. and Queen Anne periods being very rich. Not only were the faces brass, but there were to be found silvered faces also, ornamented with ormolu mounts of figures and scrolls in brass. All the space on the dial was utilized; on the extreme edge a border of leaves, or herring-bone pattern was placed, and the whole interior of the hour-ring was engraved or etched with flowers, scrolls, or set patterns, and even the winding-holes had their set of circles around each.

Of the seventeenth-century clocks the earliest had their makers' names put into Latin and engraved straight across the bottom of the dial, and quite concealed when the wooden hood of the case was in place. Later it was engraved on the lower half of the circle between the figures seven and five. These two styles were only in use very early, for about 1750 name-plates were first used, and then makers used their own taste in the matter, sometimes omitting the name entirely and substituting some motto like "Tempus Fugit" "Tempus edax rerum", and even such lengthy mottoes as the following;

"Slow comes the hour; its passing speed how great;
Waiting to seize it,—vigilantly wait!"

Edward East was another well-known early English maker, and some clocks in splendid cases came from his hand by 1690 and earlier.

Joseph Knibb and James Clowes were other popular makers about 1700. James Lownes made handsome clocks by 1705 and usually inserted glass in their doors. The corners of the dials bear devices which also point to the age of the clock. On the dials which came from the best makers till just before the close of the seventeenth century, the ornaments were cherubs' heads. Then the patterns of the spandrels, as these ornaments were called, altered, and a head set in more or less elaborate scroll-work, generally of brass, handsomely chased and often gilded, was used. After this, in the early eighteenth century, came two Cupids holding up a crown with a surrounding of scroll-work. The clock on the left in the following image has this fret, two cherubs holding a crown, at the four corners of the brass face.

Tall Case Clocks

They do not show very plainly in the illustration, which also does not do justice to the splendid marquetry with which the mahogany case is inlaid. Across the dial face is Monks, Prescot and the clock is in perfect order. The second clock is quite as interesting. It has a fine mahogany inlaid case, the face is painted on wood, the works are wooden also, and it is wound by pulling up the weights by hand. The ornaments which originally decorated the top are missing, but otherwise it is perfect and is in admirable condition. Its period is about 1800. This clock belongs to Dr. George W. Goler, of Rochester, N. Y., and the one previously described to Mr. William M. Hoyt, also of Rochester.

A crown with crossed sceptres and foliage were also used in the spandrels. Later in the century the passion for rococo ornament seized the clockmakers too, and during the reign of George III. these ornaments degenerated very greatly, and were cast brass, often not even touched with a graver's tool. Christopher Gould was making clocks in 1715, and by 1745 Richard Vick's works were put into so-called Chippendale cases. There is such a clock now at Windsor Castle.

147

All clocks before the eighteenth century had straight tops. An arched top was added, in which could be placed a register for the equation of time. On some of the latest clocks by Tompion, dated about 1709, four years before his death, such an arch is found. It is considered greatly to improve the appearance of the face of the clock, and it was utilized for decoration if not for a time register. Name-plates were put there, and a handsome dolphin was engraved or mounted on the dial on either side of the name-plate. A fine specimen of such a clock made by John Carmichael, Greenock, Scotland, and put in a mahogany case, has been owned by a family now living in Rochester, N.Y., for over one hundred and fifty years. The clock is in good order, with the original brass works, and has a small plate on the dial to indicate the day of the month. The face is silvered and etched handsomely.

During the last half of the eighteenth century there was a great demand for moving figures to be placed in this arched top. Ships in motion, Father Time, etc., were always popular subjects, as well as painted disks showing the moon in her various phases. The moving figures were preferred by Dutch makers, who excelled at this species of work. The English makers, however, used the painted moon-disks the most. The French, with their taste for the ornamental and elegant, never liked the square-faced clocks. They preferred the small clocks in ebony or alabaster casings with ormolu mounts.

Julien Le Roy was a very famous French clockmaker, whose works were mounted in florid style, sometimes in cases of kingwood, with inlay of lighter woods, or in ebony. Lepante made clocks dating from about 1750, and these were always in the best style and elegant taste. Few of such clocks found their way to America on account of their great cost.

By the last quarter of the eighteenth century watches and clocks were quite common in the colonies, where they were also made. In the "Mercury" for May 2, 1774, not only were clocks offered for sale, but

"watches neat and plain, gold, silver, shagreen, and metal. Some engraved and enamelled with devices new and elegant; also the first in this country of the small new-fashioned watches the circumference of a British shilling. John Sinnet removed to the Main St. called the Fly, next house to the corner of Beekman's slip, the sign of the dial against the wall."

In this same year Basil Francis offers;

"£1 reward for any information of a man who did in a fraudulent manner obtain one pinchbeck watch with a single case, winds up in the face, the hole where the key goes a little flowered."

There were even higher rewards offered at this time for the return of lost watches, probably not "pinchbeck," for a "military gentleman offers £5 for the return of his watch and no questions asked." The English officers made the winter of 1778-9 very gay in New York, quite rivaling Philadelphia, and set the fashion, which was esteemed very polite, of wearing two watches. The Quaker City considered this custom ridiculous. Eli Terry, of Windsor, Conn., was one of the first clockmakers in the United States, though James Harrison began to manufacture at Waterbury, Conn., as early as 1790. The first clock he made was entered in his books, "January 1, 1791, at £3 12*s.* 8*d*". Yet clocks were made even earlier than this, for in 1783 the Assembly of Connecticut awarded a patent for fourteen years to Benjamin Hanks, of Litchfield, Conn., for a self-winding clock. It was to wind itself by the help of air.

In East Windsor, Conn., Daniel Burnap carried on the manufacture of brass clocks. William Tenny was one of the earliest makers of brass work clocks in the United States, and worked at Nine Corners, Dutchess Co., N. Y. Eli Terry made wooden works for his clocks, although he had been instructed in his business by Daniel Burnap, who used brass as well as wooden works, and made tall-case clocks with long pendulums. These clocks were by no means cheap, ranging from $18 to $48, the more expensive ones having a brass dial, a dial for seconds, the moon's phases, and a better case.

Terry's wooden-work clocks were well made and were good time keepers, and were distributed all over New England by peddlers. In 1807 Terry undertook to make five hundred clocks; this overstocked the market, and he was forced to reduce the price from $25 to $15, and then to $10. Before 1800 the best-known clockmakers in the United States were Daniel Burnap, Silas Merriam, Thomas Harland, Timothy Peck, and James Harrison, all of Connecticut. From 1806 to 1815 the number of clockmakers largely increased, and Seth Thomas, Silas Hoadley, Herman Clark, and Asa Hopkins were some of the best-known men engaged in the making.

In 1814 Terry invented what was called the "short-shelf clock," in which, by a change of arrangement and smaller weights, the pendulum being brought forward and greatly shortened and the weights being carried and run on each side, the whole was reduced to a more compact form. Clock and case were sold for a moderate sum. These clocks, like the tall-case ones, were made with wooden wheels, but after the introduction of rolled brass, machinery was invented by which blank wheels could be struck out with a die, the teeth afterward cut by machinery, and the brass-wheel clocks made cheaper than the wooden. This was about 1837.

The next improvement was substituting springs for weights. This had been done in Europe for two hundred years, but only with the most costly parlour clocks, and the springs were equal to the best watch-springs. Many kinds of cheaper springs had been tried without success, till a superior steel spring was invented in the United States, and the springs thus produced have for many years been sold at a price compatible with cheap clocks.

The wooden pendulum covered with gold leaf, which is one of the characteristics of a regulator clock, was invented by Silas B. Terry, a son of Eli. America has long taken a leading place in the making of clocks, and that desire to have the biggest and best which is characteristic of the youngest nation has influenced clockmaking.

For many years England prided herself on having the largest clock in the world. It is on the Houses of Parliament, London, and is known as the Westminster clock. Its dial faces measure 22 feet 6 inches in diameter. A larger one, however, has been erected during the past few years in Minneapolis, Minn., by an American clockmaker. These dial faces measure 22 feet 8 inches in diameter, and the Westminster clock has receded to second place.

Among extraordinary clocks which have from time to time been invented, none is more curious than that made in 1767 by David Rittenhouse, of Philadelphia. It has six dials; on the main one there are four hands which indicate seconds, minutes, hours, and days, giving one day more to February in leap year. Phases of the moon are also shown. The second dial shows the movements of planets about the sun; the third, the moon revolving about the earth; the fourth, the movements of Saturn; the fifth whether sun time is fast or slow with meridian time; while the sixth gives the combination of chimes which sound quarter hours, a choice of any one of ten tunes being played by pressing a knob on the dial.

It is not often in the United States that there is a record of any piece of furniture staying in the same place for twenty-five, much less one hundred years. Yet in Westernville, Oneida Co., N. Y., there is an old "grandfather's" clock ticking away, which with the new year of 1903 is said to have stood in its present position a hundred years. The home which holds this venerable time-piece was built by General William Floyd, one of the signers of the Declaration of Independence, and the old house has weathered the storms as well as the clock. Built in the centre of a ten-thousand-acre tract of land acquired from the Indians in 1788, the lands have gradually been sold, but four hundred acres still remain surrounding the old homestead. The old mansion is well preserved, and there have been no changes beyond necessary repairs. It is of Colonial architecture, and its interior furnishings form a feast for the lovers of the antique. There are some rare pieces of furniture imported from England over a century ago. The house belongs to the widow of Admiral Sicard, and was left her by her father, the grandson of General Floyd.

Of the tall-case clocks there were many to be found all over the South, in some instances case and all being brought from England, while in others, as was often done, the case was made by the local cabinet-maker. Many such clocks have, within recent years, found their way into Newport, R. I., which is quite a paradise for the antiquarian. The history of these old clocks is strange. During the Civil War the negroes appropriated many articles from the manor houses which had been deserted, or partially sacked or burned, and carried them to their cabins. Among such loot were many clocks, but they were too tall to get into the cabin doors or to stand upright afterward. So they were cut down, generally at the base, for the ornamental tops, particularly if there were brass ornaments on the top, appealed to their new owners. A dealer from Newport heard of them, and went to Virginia, buying all of these sawed off clocks he could find. He took them home, had the cases restored, and sold them all for good prices.

One of the most famous names in the history of clock making in America is that of Willard, and to a certain style of clock this name has been applied. There were at least four clockmakers by this name, Simon, Aaron, Benjamin, and Simon Jr. It is supposed to be the latter who made the style of clock also known as "banjo," although Mr. Lockwood considers there is great doubt on the subject. One of these clocks is shown in the earlier three centuries image. They had no striking machinery, and often varied as to the lower part, occasionally being furnished with a brass ornament. This one has a view of Mt. Vernon, and belonged to the late Mr. Alfred Hosmer, of Concord, Mass. These clocks were made during the first twenty years of the nineteenth century. The works are of brass and generally of excellent make.

Mantel Clocks

In 1802 "Willard of Boston," who was, no doubt, Benjamin, who had workshops at Roxbury and Grafton as well as in Boston, took out a patent for his timepieces. At this same period Terry began business on a larger scale and by water-power. In 1814 he introduced the shelf or mantel-clock, which he patented in 1816. Three of this style of clock are shown in the image on the previous page. All are in good condition and are still running. They belong to Mr. William M. Hoyt, of Rochester, N. Y.

The central clock is a very handsome one of mahogany, with a carved case. The ornament on the top is an eagle, and the posts are leaves bound with a rope. The face of Washington painted on the glass is much better than those portraits usually are, and loses much in the reproduction. This clock was made by Ephraim Downs, of Bristol, Conn. The clock on the left, made by Chauncey Ives, is also a Bristol one, for Connecticut early obtained and has always retained an eminence in the clock business. It has an ornamental case with handsomely carved pineapples on top, and a swan-necked cornice. The one on the right, with claw feet, has a very handsome decoration of painted patterns on a black ground. On the inner part of the case is pasted a paper which reads as follows:

"PATENT CLOCKS
PATENTED BY ELI TERRY

151

AND MADE AND SOLD BY SETH THOMAS
PLYMOUTH MASS. WARRANTED IF WELL USED."

The faces of all three are painted on tin, the two Bristol clocks having ornamentation of gold in the corners. These clocks all date from 1815-20, but the one by Seth Thomas may be a trifle earlier.

A more modern clock than any of the foregoing, yet one of interest, nevertheless, is one in the commandant's office in the Navy Yard, Brooklyn. This old clock, which, although fifty-four years old, is not only in good running order, but practically furnishes the official time for the yard, occupies a prominent position in the outer office of Rear-Admiral Barker's suite. Its dial is about the same size as those seen in the clocks of to-day that keep the official time, but it is operated by a spring instead of weights. Its mahogany case is handsomely carved, and its brass hands shine in a way that shows the care that it receives. The following inscription, revealing the age of the clock, appears on the case:

PRESENTED TO THE
U. S. FRIGATE BRANDYWINE,
BY THE CREW, 1849.

No one in the yard knows how the old clock got there,—it probably drifted there, as have so many other waifs and strays. At noon every day it is set by official time received from the Naval Observatory in Washington, and most of the other clocks in the yard depend upon this reliable time-piece which has come down from the frigate "Brandywine."

The collecting of clocks is a fad which few people indulge in. Yet there are those who own ten or a dozen timepieces, and who like to have them in running order. The old Dutch clocks, while looking very well, are notoriously ill-regulated time-keepers. A collector took a prize lately acquired to an old German clock-repairer who seemed more learned in the ways of ancient clocks than many a more pretentious maker. The clock did not come home when it was promised, and the owner went to see what was the matter. She found her old clockmaker diligently studying a little German volume with a title which read something like this, "Thirteen Hundred Reasons why a Clock in Perfect Order Won't Run."

Furniture Handles, Feet and Miscellany

IN the manufacture of furniture at one time or another nearly every variety of wood has been used, if not for the body of the frame, then for its enrichment, and every quarter of the globe has been laid under contribution. The island of Borneo yielded Amboyna wood, with its beautiful mottlings and curlings, and a very splendid cabinet was made of it for the ill-fated Marie Antoinette by the famous cabinet-maker of her day, Riesener. Ceylon, held by the Dutch as a colony from the middle of the seventeenth century until nearly the nineteenth, produced splendid ebony which was used for whole pieces of furniture as well as for decoration. The French term *ébéniste*, or worker in ebony, was given to the French makers of fine work.

Kitchen of Whipple House, Ipswich, Massachusetts

To what abundant usage oak, walnut, and mahogany was put we know. Rosewood, too, was another of the choicer materials. Satin-wood, with its brilliant colour; tulip-wood, more showy still; kingwood, dark and rich; zebra wood, with its black and white effect, as well as leopard and partridge woods,— were all in use before 1800. There were, besides, cherry, yew, pear, walnut, cedar, fir, olive, beech, sycamore, cypress, chestnut for timber work, poplar, acacia, with limewood and boxwood for carving.

For furniture which was to be painted and gilded common deal was used. In America hickory (nut-wood, as it was called), was very popular among the native workers, and all the other woods were gradually imported, except those used for inlaying, an art never much practiced by American cabinet makers.

After the first leather coverings of cured bull-hide there followed Spanish or Cordova leather, Turkey-work, cane, rush, tapestry, brocade, woollen plush, etc., as styles altered from time to time and luxury increased. In an earlier chapter mention has been made of stuffs that were in use in the seventeenth and eighteenth centuries for bed and window curtains, draperies and upholstery. Besides all the varieties of English goods, large importations came from East India of such unfamiliar materials, as bejurapants bafts, gorgorans, mulmuls, jainwars, sallampores, and many others.

Miss Singleton in her "Furniture of Our Forefathers," gives a list of eighty different stuffs, seersuckers being the only familiar name among them. Presumably some of these were imported here, and Boston merchants before 1725 advertised linceys and flowered serges, bangalls, shalloons, Persians and fustian, kersey, silk crêpes, cherry derry and grass. Worsted, or hair plush, plain or striped hair-cloth, damask, furniture dimities, moreen, harrateen and tammy were all to be bought in the larger cities. Nor were these goods by any means cheap. Harrateen cost about four dollars a yard in the middle of the eighteenth century, and a set of curtains of this same material was valued at $210. Other goods were in

Drop Handle
1675-1700

Early Willow Pattern.
1720-1760

Bail Handle.
1760-1785

Pressed Brass Oval.
1780-1810

Rosette and Ring
1790-1820

Inset Ring
1800

Rosette
1820

Handles, Escutheons, etc.

proportion; some bedsteads without beds coming as high as $100. But, once acquired, these household goods were valuable assets and passed from one generation to another, often mentioned with great particularity by will.

There are various small details which are of assistance in determining the approximate period of a piece of furniture, and none of greater value than the handles. The different styles of these, particularly of brass, are quite definite. The earliest of them is the drop handle, shown in the picture to follow, and also on the old oak chest depicted at the beginning of this book. The escutcheons were similar, and the material of the drops on some chests of drawers was iron, but brass was more commonly seen, and was either hollow or solid.

154

After the drop handles followed bail handles of a primitive type, the handles being fastened in with wires. These handles also were of brass and were sometimes engraved. The shape of these handles and escutcheons is known as willow, and appears later in a much more ornate form. See Figures 56, 57 and 59. By this time the handles were fastened by screw and nut. By the latter half of the eighteenth century there were in addition to the elaborate willow brasses oval ones of various styles. This shape was much affected by Hepplewhite on his sideboards, and by Sheraton in his earlier style (see Figures 35 and 38).

There was a handle starting from two small plates, either round or oval, frequently seen on swell-front bureaus and desks of 1780 and thereabouts. One is shown in the following image. Beginning at the top of the page the various handles in use in the eighteenth century are shown in the order of their appearance.

There was also a round handle with a ring lying close within it; and when the Empire style was in favour a rosette with a ring was used on sideboards, bureaus, writing-tables, etc. See Figures 42 and 60. The rosette with a ring was not the only Empire style, but there were round knob handles of brass, glass and brass with medallions of china or enamel. The glass ones, either transparent or opalescent, were held in great esteem, though they are extremely ugly on pieces of dark furniture on which they were usually mounted. In many cases they have been removed, and wooden knobs substituted; yet if one desires an Empire piece to look as it did when made, it will be necessary to hunt out, if possible, a set of these knobs to put on it. This is not so difficult a matter as might be imagined; for even if the handles come from divers places they will generally match, as there was small variety in the patterns used.

There was a great demand for these opal glass rosettes. Very large ones held back the window curtains, smaller ones were used to support the mirrors, besides those on the furniture. About this same time (1820) those fine handles which are so eagerly sought for to-day made their appearance. They were china or enamel set in brass, and the patterns on the china were often portraits of famous men like Washington, Franklin, Clinton, and Jefferson. When mounted on a piece of furniture like a small work-table, which had only two drawers, the four patriots named would make a set. There were also fancy heads, and sometimes tiny figures, but these were not so popular.

Brass was put to many other uses, ornamental as well as useful, and wine-coolers of heavy mahogany were set off with bands of it, and smaller articles, like pipkins, were either made or bound with it. Narrow thread-like bands of brass were used for purposes of inlay and in the lyre-back chairs the strings were brass, as well as the accompanying ornaments. Brass has always been a valuable commodity in English manufactures, and in the reign of Henry VIII. Parliament passed an act prohibiting, under severe penalties, the export of brass, which prohibition was not withdrawn till as recently as 1799. In 1721 over thirty thousand persons were employed in brass-founding in Birmingham, England, and the business has grown until it has become the industrial feature of that city.

The handles of both French and Dutch furniture were extremely ornate, consisting of scrolls and leaves, many of them of great beauty and delicacy, particularly when made of water-gilt or of etched brass.

For the benefit of local cabinet-makers brass handles, escutcheons, and false keyholes were imported and on sale in America. By 1770 many cabinet-makers were manufacturing very handsome furniture of mahogany, cedar, or cherry, requiring handsome brasses to go with them. A cabinet-maker of Newburyport, R. I., had in his shop at the time of his death in 1773 much furniture completed and some still unfinished. He also had several thousand feet of costly timber, sixty brass handles valued at more than one pound, desk brasses, fifty-four escutcheons, and old brasses, locks, and screws as well. For bookcase and cabinet doors he had panes of glass, most of it in sheets measuring 5 × 7 inches, which was the size commonly used in windows at that time. Although glass had been made in this country for a long time we find "Bristol crown window-glass" advertised for sale in 1771 in sizes as large as 9 × 12 inches.

Besides these brasses of English manufacture, we find another merchant advertising "three dozen Dutch rings and escutcheons at three shillings a dozen." Handles came at various prices, fifteen, twelve, and eight shillings a dozen, according to pattern and finish. The escutcheons were at proportionate prices, eleven and eight shillings a dozen, but locks came high, a fine-ward desk-lock bringing a guinea.

On much furniture, particularly that enriched with inlay, ivory escutcheons were used, and sometimes those holly or other wood used in the inlay were set in. These were in use during the last years of the eighteenth century, and can be found in connection with various styles of handles.

At the "Smith's Fly" were many metal-workers who sold ironware and goods for cabinet-makers. At the sign of the "Cross Daggers," Thomas Brown, as early as 1745, had many metal furnishings on hand. There were latches and bolts for doors and locks for chests, drawers, and cabinets. He had polished brass handles, locks, escutcheons, and handsome brass locks for parlours. Ring-drops, tea-chest furniture, knobs and knockers for street doors, curtain-rings and chafing-dishes were advertised in 1750, and casters and handles and escutcheons of the newest fashion were to be found in 1751, with brass chair nails.

A few years later double and single spring chest-locks could be bought, and these were sold by the same merchant who imported—

—"choice India and Japan gilded Tea Tables, square Dressing ditto, of which sort none were ever seen in America before."

The rate to be charged for putting on these brasses was set down in "The Journeymen's Cabinet and Chair-makers Philadelphia Book of Prices," 1795, mentioned before. Common castors cost 2½d each, and 1d extra for letting in the plate; a set of sockets "when the legs are tapered, to fit in, per set," 1s 2d. Iron or brass rollers were 8½d per pair. Fitting on a box lock was 1s 4d, while a patent lock came extra and cost 2s. Lifting handles could be put on for 1s 4d per pair. Letting in an escutcheon was 2½d for each one, and letting in plates for rods in the tops of sideboards were 8d for each plate. Ivory escutcheons cost 10d each, and those of holly just half that.

If a person chose to have his furniture made on the premises it was an easy matter, for many cabinet-makers worked in this way, and the furniture could be built to suit exactly the prospective owner's taste and the place it was to occupy. None of the furniture made in America and little that was imported here, had the superb handles and escutcheons which were put on French and Dutch pieces. These mounts were executed and designed by artists, and made a decidedly beautiful addition to the furniture.

Another distinctive feature of old furniture is the foot, which in many cases points to period and country as well as if the piece was dated. After the turned chairs with their heavy lines and clumsy construction, the furniture which was gradually finding its way from Spain and Holland seemed very beautiful. The Flemish foot, so called, turns outward, and is found on very early chairs enriched with carving and having cane, rush, or turkey-work seats. This style belongs to the last quarter of the seventeenth century.

Chairs of this same period also came from Spain and Portugal, being covered with the splendid leather of Cordova, which has now a world-wide reputation. The woodwork of the frames was handsome enough to correspond with the leather. These frames were carved, and the foot turned out like the Flemish, but it was of quite a different shape and fluted (see Figure 100).

This Spanish foot retained its popularity a long time, appearing on many varieties of chairs almost as late as 1750. It was associated with cane, rush, leather, and stuff bottoms, was seen on arm and side chairs with slatted backs, and backs of cane and leather. Sometimes on the "roundabout chairs," as those having a square seat set with one angle pointed forward were called only the front foot was in Spanish style, the others being turned knobs which accorded with the turned legs and rails. Even on some of the so-called Queen Anne chairs with spoon backs, a modified form of Spanish foot was to be found, but this eventually gave way to the familiar ball-and-claw cabriole leg, or the regular Dutch foot. It is curious that the cabriole leg with ball-and-claw foot was seen on pieces of furniture like both the high and low chests of drawers before it was used on chairs and the earliest of these Queen Anne chairs had the bandy leg with the plain Dutch foot. This foot is used with the solid splat and the spoon-shaped back with rounded ends to the top.

Chippendale, in his earliest work, began to use the models then in vogue, and, with the bandy leg which was found only on the two front legs of chairs, used also a modified Dutch foot. Very soon he used instead the ball-and-claw foot, with or without the underbrace, and with the more ornamental foot the splat became pierced and carved and very ornate and rich. The later straight legged Chippendale chair (see Chapter III) came into favour, with or without underbraces, and late in the eighteenth century the other great cabinet-makers came along, each with his distinctive styles and characteristics. The first of these is Hepplewhite, who never achieved the success of Chippendale, who preceded him, nor of Sheraton, who succeeded him, yet whose work is often very beautiful. He did not, of course confine himself to any one style of foot or leg, yet on many of his chairs, tables, and sideboards he used what is called the "spade foot." This was varied in many ways, but the most common form is shown in the following image.

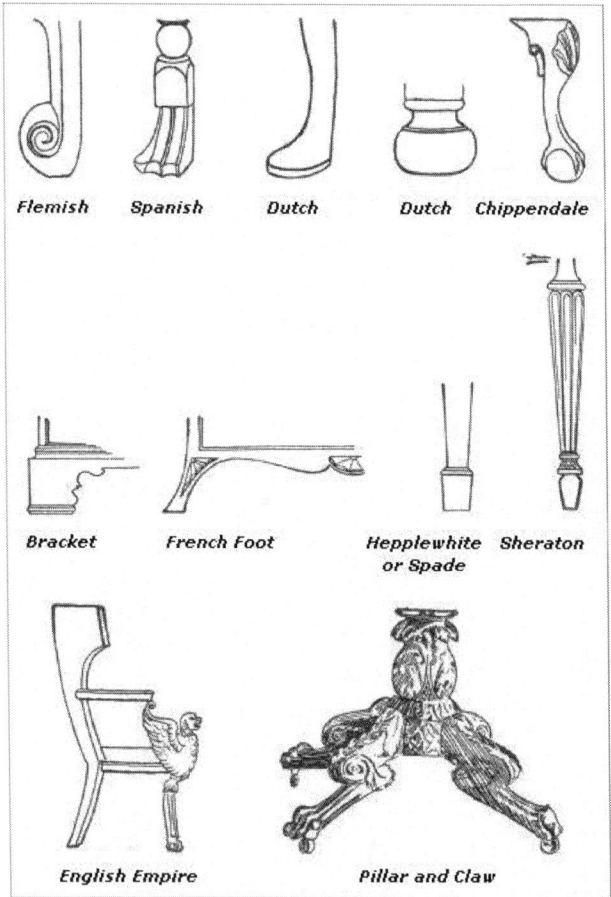

Flemish   Spanish   Dutch   Dutch   Chippendale

Bracket   French Foot   Hepplewhite   Sheraton
or Spade

English Empire   Pillar and Claw

Both Hepplewhite and Sheraton, as well as the other makers of the eighteenth century, used a variety of shapes of feet, for bureaus, desks, bookcases, and other pieces which were in no way distinctive. Each maker used the bracket foot as suited him best, adding curves to suit his fancy or the exigencies of the case, or inlay or even carving. A plain bracket foot is also shown in the picture. The French foot is more ornate and slender, and comes on chests of drawers, bureaus, etc. Inlay is very often used for its decoration, and it adds a graceful line to the piece it is used on, which is always of choice wood inlaid or painted.

158

The tapering fluted foot which we associate with Sheraton is also shown in the picture. Under his treatment it was nearly always decorated, either inlaid or carved, or sometimes both. Although we are most familiar with Sheraton style furniture in mahogany, he made much other furniture besides, as the following description of drawing-room chairs shows:

"These drawing-room chairs are finished in white and gold, or the ornaments may be japanned, but the French finish them in mahogany with gilt mouldings. The figures in the tablets above the front rails are on French printed silk or satin, sewed onto the stuffing with borders round them. The seat and back are of the same kind, as is the ornamented tablet at the top of the chair. The top rail is pannelled, a small gold bead mitred round, and the printed silk pasted on. Chairs of this kind have an effect which far exceeds any conception we can have of them from an uncoloured engraving, or even a coloured one."

This does not seem like the furniture we know as "Sheraton", yet in his books are many similar descriptions. After Sheraton gave up manufacturing furniture, and wrote only books of descriptions and patterns, France had passed through the throes of the Revolution, when the old *régime* was swept away. Napoleon had been proclaimed First Consul, and then, in 1802, confirmed for life, and took under his charge even such minor details as furniture and dress. The styles arranged to suit his whim found an echo in England. The English Empire, both at its best and worse estate, could boast of nothing better than a feeble imitation of the antique, while the French Empire was at least an expression of the conquests and successes of one man.

Thomas Hope was perhaps the best exponent of this style in England, and he industriously mingled emblems of the gods and goddesses, Phrygian caps and Roman fasces, Greek amphoræ, and fabulous animals on the furniture which he designed. In Figure 100 is shown one side of a chair designed by him, as also an Empire pillar-and-claw leg, as rendered by American cabinet-makers. Less ornate and ambitious, the American treatment of this period is preferable, for the chief use to which they put brass and bronze, the too-abundant use of which was so characteristic of this style, was to tip columns or pillars, and, to some extent, the feet of tables.

The best old furniture which is to be found in the United States is of this period, which was succeeded by what may be denominated the black-walnut age, the chief characteristic of which was abundant coarse carving. Our cabinet-makers were very successful in their treatment of mahogany, both solid and veneered. The latter work has never been excelled, and shows its perfection by the good condition in which much of this furniture, seventy and eighty years old, is found to-day.

The smaller affairs of life which go to make up the sum of necessaries were woefully wanting in the households of pioneers who battled with the American wilderness. The importance of the iron pot, weighing thirty or forty pounds, which descended by will through three or four generations, has already been pointed out.

Pewter and brass ware were equally esteemed, and pewter, while by no means expensive, was not so plentiful but that many people managed with a small supply. Pewter spoons bent and broke, and a substitute, at least in the Connecticut Valley, was a small clam-shell set in a cleft stick. However much pewter was owned, whenever the Revolutionary heroes called for bullets, what there was was cheerfully run into those missiles of war, and there were many "bees" held all through the Colonies where bullets were run, and wooden trenchers were whittled out by the young lads to take the place of the sacrificed pewter. This wooden ware later was smoothed down by the women of the household with broken glass, and polished with sand made of powdered limestone.

Some of these wooden articles, made of maple, poplar or apple-wood, have descended to show with what simple appliances our ancestors were content. How simple were their pleasures the records of the time show. In fact, anything so enlivening as a hanging was looked upon as sport for a holiday. The first State's prison was opened in 1797 at the foot of Tenth Street, New York city. It was in use for thirty years, till the structure at Sing Sing superseded it. Grant Thorburn, referring to a man who was reprieved through the efforts of the Society of Friends, writes as follows:

"One day I went up to the park to see a man hung. After gazing two hours at the gallows, the sheriff announced a reprieve. I must own I was disappointed."

Though amusements and pleasures were few, even such as came along could not well be enjoyed if the weather were stormy, and in Washington's diary the entry for November 29, 1789, is, "Being very snowy, not a single person appeared at the Levee." Clothes could not be risked; they were too valuable to be subjected to bad weather. Romalls, amens, casserillias, and ribdilures were high-sounding but perishable. Even while luxury was considered, health was neglected in many ways, such valuable adjuncts as tooth-brushes not being in use until about 1782.

Many advertisements appear in the papers of men who combined several vocations, dentistry being one of them, and in 1789 General Washington, after much pain during the summer, went into the hands of John Greenwood, dentist, of 56 William Street, New York, who made him a set of "sea-horse teeth". This had been a very trying summer, and one newspaper has it that "raw rum has been found exceeding pernicious in this extreme," and something lighter, like a "Bishop" or "Lawn sleeves" was recommended, and study of a book published in England called "Oxford Night-caps" was suggested as furnishing recipes for various healthful beverages though it was added that the rum had better be omitted, "as it is very intoxicating, and therefore pernicious."

The President's guests could choose from among Madeira, claret, champagne, sherry, arrack, spirits, brandy, cordials, porter, beer, and cider, yet, with it all, unseemly intoxication seems to have been the exception.

Domestic discipline in New York was enforced on servants, whether bound or free, by means of an official who was stationed at the calaboose on the common, and who, for a fee of one shilling, gave a thorough whipping. Education was fostered and colleges throve. By 1760 the records state that the "King's College (Columbia) buildings were so far completed that the officers and students began to lodge and mess therein."

This was in accordance with the terms of the charter, which further provided that the students were to wear caps and gowns and to be within the gates at a certain hour. The plan of education, like our belongings, was copied from England, and our college was, in the most material parts, to be like Queen's College, Oxford. The tuition fee when General Washington entered his step-son, John Parke Custis, there, was five pounds per annum, with room-rent four pounds, and board at the rate of eleven shillings weekly.

The late Andrew P. Peabody, writing of college life at Harvard in 1820, says:

"Coal, just then coming into use, had hardly found its way into college. The student's rooms, several of the recitation-rooms as well were heated by open fires. Friction matches, which according to Faraday were the most useful invention in our age, were not yet."

He says that the feather-bed was a valuable asset (this article had held its own for centuries), but that ten dollars would have covered the other contents of a student's room. It had no carpet, and a pine bedstead, a washstand, table and desk, and three or four chairs were all it contained, besides a cannon-ball to be heated on extra-cold nights, and rolled down stairs on warm ones, "at such time as might most nearly bisect a proctor's night's sleep."

Our maternal great-great-grandmothers must have had little leisure to spare from the duties that occupied their time. Yet many of them had still-rooms where they not only compounded the medicaments whereby many a family was raised from infancy, but where they made extracts and essences as well. They made, too, from the flowers and herbs that grew in their gardens, pomander-balls, which were used instead of vinaigrettes, the outer case being of silver or gold, and often as large as an orange.

Those whose stock of trinkets did not boast one of these metal cases used the rind of an orange, the inside being carefully extracted, and a sponge with vinegar and spices being inserted in its place. Rose-balls made of leaves beaten to pulp, mixed with sweet spices, and rolled into a ball, soon became hard, resembling the rosaries made in the south of France. When held in the hand they became very fragrant from its warmth. Simpler than any of these was a rosy apple stuck full of cloves and giving out a fragrance years after the apple had lost all appearance or consistency of being a fruit, and awakening in the mind an image of her who made it in some quiet garden long ago.

Conclusion

All this antique furniture that we have passed in review has an aroma of its own compounded by the hand that built it, the person that owned it, and the scenes that it has lived through. The anecdotes which they attracted in their wake have an equal level of importance, in that they confer a living history which in many cases enhances the significance of their respective item.

Many a sober old chair could discourse of experiences ranging from sorrowful to joyous, from lively to severe, and every one of these antiques, whether a treasured heirloom or a reclaimed derelict, has a charm that is not easily excelled. Discoveries from the eras depicted do however appear regularly in both the USA and Europe, offering hope to the enthused collector who might happen upon a furnishing they suspect as a specimen mentioned within these pages.

While there remains a multitude of collectible and valued furnishings in addition to those featured in the pages of this book, the principles espoused remain constant. Observe the extremities of the item as signifier of its value and authenticity, and absorb the past as an eager historian so that customers and associates alike may admire your ability to wax lyrical on the history surrounding a given piece.

Given how deep this book has delved, it goes without saying that antique discovery and trade is firmly within the category of savoured esoteric. It is my wish that you utilise the information offered here to great effect, becoming a better discoverer and enthusiast, inflaming the passion which drove this text's very compilation.

Printed in Great Britain
by Amazon

32238162R00092